A Month-by-Month Guide to
Organic Gardening

A comprehensive guide to growing your own fruit and vegetables
sucessfully, using nature's own resources to enrich the soil and
combat pests and diseases.

A Month-by-Month Guide to

ORGANIC GARDENING

A month-by-month guide to managing an Organic Garden

by

Lawrence D. Hills

Illustrated by Piotr Swierczynski

THORSONS PUBLISHERS LIMITED
Wellingborough, Northamptonshire

First published 1983

British Library Cataloguing in Publication Data

Hills, Lawrence D.
    A month-by-month guide to organic gardening.
    1. Organic gardening
    I. Title
    635'.0484   SB453.5

    ISBN 0-7225-0795-X

Printed and bound in Great Britain

Contents

Foreword

In an age when so much money and effort is expended on the advertising and selling of chemical fertilizers and of newer pesticides, the survival and growth of the Organic Movement is a remarkable phenomenon.

Lawrence Hills has played a unique role in that survival and growth. He has the rare gift, as a scientist, of being able – in simple language and striking metaphor – to make his science intelligible to the non-scientist.

In his lectures, travels, writings and by the founding of the Henry Doubleday Research Association he has carried the torch of organic gardening throughout Britain and to other lands. The HDRA has three groups in Australia, one in New Zealand, another in India, and a sixth recently established in Sri Lanka.

For struggling organic gardeners like me, his books are a godsend; they comprise a veritable mine of valuable information and above all of practical advice.

This new book is written for those who seek more knowledge of the nutritive value of garden crops and who wish to grow their own fruit and vegetables for the health of their families.

There is sound evidence suggesting that much ill health in Britain, including certain birth defects, is due to mineral and vitamin deficiencies. Year by year new evidence accumulates of the vitally important part played by green leaf and fresh food vitamins such as folic acid and ascorbic acid in maintaining normal bodily function. It is probably true that we have grossly underestimated the daily requirement of these and other vitamins.

We eat far too much refined sugar and white flour. These worthless, deprived foods displace natural foods – fruit, vegetables and whole-grain cereals – and so we suffer all the dire effects of vitamin, mineral and fibre deficiency, and from what T.L. Cleave termed 'over-consumption'.

As a nation we are constipated, our hospital waiting lists are loaded with hundreds of patients suffering from the complications of that distressing condition. Our national health will not improve until we discard worthless 'industrialized foods' and return to nature's own food, prepared with the minimum of human manipulation.

Readers of *Organic Gardening All the Year Round* will find a clear exposition of the botanical grouping of fruits and vegetables and details of their mineral and vitamin content. A masterful review of various methods of compost making is followed by a month-by-month account of the organic garden. We are carried along by the author's enthusiasm which has the effect of making us eager to rush out and 'get on with it'.

This book will inspire established organic gardeners to improve their methods and encourage newcomers to begin. It will do more for the health of the nation than much medicine.

Walter W. Yellowlees
MC, MB, Ch.B., FRCGP

Preface

I have written this book to help those who have health problems to garden their way out of them, for the healthiest of all health foods are those grown without chemicals in your own garden. In particular I am thinking of those with allergies or on special diets of all kinds, for whom the right food is better than any medicine. Therefore this book includes many tables of vitamins, minerals, and other substances of nutritional value, taken mainly from *The Composition of Foods* by R.A. McCance and E. M. Widdowson (HMSO, 1960) and *Bridges Food and Beverage Analysis* by Marjorie R. Mattice (Henry Kimpton, 1950). The figures relating to the least usual vegetables and many others are by Dr A.H. Ward, Analyst to the Henry Doubleday Research Association. Other sources are acknowledged in the text.

Firstly, I would like to thank Dr William Yellowlees, President of the McCarrison Society, for his Foreword. I would also thank the Editor of *Garden News* for permission to use material that has appeared in my fortnightly organic gardening column. I would express my appreciation of the work of Piotr Swierczynski, formerly an HDRA student, for the line drawings that illustrate this book.

Finally, I must thank my wife, Hilda Cherry Hills, who knows far more about food than I do, for her help, her suggestions and her corrections. Books, like gardens, are always better when they are family affairs.

Lawrence D. Hills

1.

The Organic Gardener's Year

The gardener's year starts slowly with seed catalogues and planning in January, but all too soon the tide of spring comes racing in over the shallow weeks, sweeping up to midsummer and ebbing slowly away to autumn and winter. Our crops have 'gardening diaries' inside them, kept by the changing length of the days, and when cold, dry springs hold them back, while the day length drives them on, they race ahead when the warm rain comes at last, until you can almost hear the whisper of their growth below the shouting of the weeds.

We feed the soil with organic manures and fertilizers, which wait for the sun to warm the living soil to life, so our crops start more slowly than those of our inorganic neighbours, whose chemicals are quicker, but ours catch up and finish with finer flavours and qualities that all organic gardeners know. Time matters more to us because we follow our crops rather than drive them.

This book is written to help organic gardeners keep up with the tides of the racing year, for so much of the art of using time to make space go further, and controlling pests and diseases by cunning rather than chemicals, depends on making the right choice among the jobs that clamour to be done before the light fades and another weekend is gone. It is more important to sow, plant or thin with the tide of life, than to mow and edge and tidy. It is less important to do the job very well, or neatly, than to do it at the right time when you are a beginner. With experience comes the ability to work both fast and well, as you learn the speed without haste that has fed the peasants of the world through the centuries.

Crop rotation

Not only do we need to take our crops round the year to bring us food for all seasons. We must take them round the garden so that each one helps the crop that follows, leaving the maximum interval to rest the soil and allow the disease spores and pests to die out rather than build up trouble for the future. The usual garden rotation is one of four beds, with potatoes, root crops, cabbage tribe and pea tribe following each other, so that it is four years before each group of crops grows in the same place.

Bed 1
Potatoes:
    Earlies, followed by leeks.
    Maincrop, followed by broad beans.

Bed 2
Legumes:
    Broad beans
    Peas
    Runner beans
    French beans
    Haricot beans
All peas and beans followed by young plants of Brussels sprouts, sprouting broccoli, cabbage.

Bed 3
Brassicas:
    Cabbage tribe, planted as young plants in this bed the year
        before.
    Outdoor tomatoes after the winter cabbages are cleared.
    Lettuces, radishes, turnips or swedes.

Bed 4
Roots:
   Onions
   Carrots
   Beet
   Kohl rabi
   Salsify
   Parsnips
   Lettuces

Pests and diseases that can be controlled or prevented by rotation almost always follow families, and there are many of these with so few pests or diseases that they need not be rotated but fitted in wherever there is room. Lettuces, which belong to the daisy family *(Compositae)*, are an example. These and others in the same useful class are marked with an asterisk in Table 1. Those whose gardens are too small to grow enough potatoes to be worth the trouble could replace these with a bed of lettuce and the other salad crops that do not need rotation, while in very small gardens, especially those filled with clubroot spores by previous owners, it is possible to forget about rotations and grow only crops that do not need this method. If you merely cut out the potatoes and make yours a three-bed rotation, you are bringing the onions and cabbages back to the same place too soon.

The pea tribe
Members of the pea tribe have nitrogen-fixing bacteria in their roots, and organic gardeners sow as many of these as possible, to grow their own fertilizer rather than buying it in bags. Adding an extra bed of white-seeded runners for drying as butter or haricot beans gives extra concentrated storable protein, of value to vegetarians and those who wish to grow as much as possible of their food in their own gardens, as well as even more nitrogen. Gardens with poor soil can be built up by adding a bed under 'green manure crops', which are usually nitrogen-fixers. After sowing they grow with relatively little trouble and can be dug in to build up fertility.

You cannot safely grow *only* the pea tribe, for this can build up a number of harmful soil fungi, as every construction-minded gardener finds when he concretes in permanent metal-piping 'goal post' structure to string his runner beans along. The spores of plant diseases dry and blow on the wind, can be carried on shoes and, in the case of clubroot, arrive on the roots of bought-in plants or manure. Generally speaking it is safest to think of your 'no-star' crops as like lightning– they should never strike the same place twice.

Potato eelworm cysts (white, yellow, or brown pinheads on the roots of plants that are stunted and giving smaller and smaller crops each year) and microscopic clubroot spores last up to nine years in the soil. Onion downy-mildew spores live on in roots and dug-in foliage for at least four years, and with the rising popularity of autumn-sown onions and perennials like the Welsh onion, this disease is increasing, and so is onion white rot. The strongest argument against the old garden custom of making up a permanent onion bed with plenty of soot, bonemeal and sulphate of potash, is the stem eelworm, *Dithylenchus dipsaci*, which causes onion bloat, with plants swelling at the base, leaves swollen and distorted, and cracked and rotting bulbs. This non-cyst-forming eelworm can also attack phlox in the herbaceous border and migrate to strawberries and parsnips, causing the same bloated and distorted stems and rotting of the crop.

The answer to these and many other soil problems is crop rotation, ideally longer than the usual four years. If you have room for it, a six-bed system is excellent: add a bed resting under green manures, or extra pea-tribe crops, and bring the strawberry bed into the rotation. The alternative is to cut down on the cabbage tribe if you have increasing clubroot trouble, keeping to the winter and spring crops like sprouting broccoli, and grow only early potatoes and spring-sown onions to reduce the build-up, a process helped by plenty of good compost, for all diseases are worst in chemically fed gardens.

Make your own rotation

Few gardeners want to grow every vegetable there is, and the best way of saving space is to grow only what you eat and enjoy. Therefore every garden needs its own rotation, which can be altered to suit changing tastes and by discarding failures, a process of experiment and adventure that is one of the many joys of gardening. Composing your own rotation needs knowledge of the tribes, or natural orders, of our crops. Pests and diseases run in families, like many other qualities. The vegetables in this book belong to thirteen natural orders, fifteen if you count the

Labiatae, to which most herbs belong, and the *Rosaceae*, the rose family, which includes apples, pears, raspberries and strawberries. Only the last named need rotation.

Natural orders

The system of Natural Orders was devised by Carl Von Linne of Sweden (1707-78) (who called himself 'Linnaeus' because he used Latin which was then the international language of science), and recorded in his great work that has made the study of the living world possible. In an age that is likely to think that Plato is a washing-up liquid, the Latin names may be awkward for many gardeners, so they have been numbered for ease of reference, as given at the bottom of Table 1. The most important to remember in planning rotations are: No. 4 – the *Cruciferae*, the Brassicas or cabbage family; No. 7 – the *Leguminosae* or pea tribe; No. 8 – the *Liliaceae, the onions,* and No. 11 – the *Solanaceae,* to which potatoes, tomatoes, sweet peppers and aubergines belong.

Table 1: Vegetables in their orders

Artichokes* (Jerusalem)	*Compositae*	Miner's lettuce*	*Portulacaceae*
Beans	*Leguminosae*	New Zealand spinach*	*Aizoaceae*
Beet*	*Chenopodiaceae*	Onions	*Liliaceae*
Broccoli	*Cruciferae*	Parsley	*Umbelliferae*
Brussels sprouts	*Cruciferae*	Parsnips	*Umbelliferae*
Cabbages	*Cruciferae*	Peas	*Leguminosae*
Carrots	*Umbelliferae*	Potatoes	*Solanaceae*
Cauliflowers	*Cruciferae*	Pumpkins*	*Cucurbitaceae*
Celeriac	*Umbelliferae*	Radishes	*Cruciferae*
Celery	*Umbelliferae*	Rhubarb*	*Polygonaceae*
Cucumbers*	*Cucurbitaceae*	Salsify*	*Compositae*
Hamburg parsley	*Umbelliferae*	Savoys	*Cruciferae*
Kale	*Cruciferae*	Scorzonera*	*Compositae*
Kohl rabi	*Cruciferae*	Shallots	*Liliaceae*
Lamb's lettuce*	*Valerianaceae*	Spinach	*Chenopodiaceae*
Landcress*	*Cruciferae*	Swedes	*Cruciferae*
Leeks	*Liliaceae*	Sweetcorn	*Gramineae*
Lettuces*	*Compositae*	Tomatoes	*Solanaceae*
Marrows*	*Cucurbitaceae*	Turnips	*Cruciferae*

Natural orders by number

Aizoaceae	1		*Liliaceae*	8
Chenopodiaceae	2		*Polygonaceae*	9
Compositae	3		*Portulacaceae*	10
Cruciferae	4		*Solanaceae*	11
Cucurbitaceae	5		*Umbelliferae*	12
Gramineae	6		*Valerianaceae*	13
Leguminosae	7			

Though there are only thirty-eight vegetables on this list, they have many varieties and it is their earliness, lateness and the length of time a single sowing stays in production that makes our gardens feed us so long and so well. There are about 300 varieties of potato, which include early – to dig and scrape first in July or even June, and second early – like Duke of York, which can be scraped as an early and dug to keep far into the spring when it grows large and is tasty baked in its jacket in September, leaving a better choice of winter crops to follow it than the maincrops which produce the highest yields, lifted in October.

The variety problem
It is no longer possible for any gardening writer to recommend varieties for flavour and garden qualities and be sure that they will be available to readers by the time the book is in print. Under the Plant Varieties and Seeds Act of 1964, as amended by the European Communities Act of 1972 and enforced by the Seeds (National Lists of Varieties) Regulations of 1 July 1973, it is an offence, punishable by a fine of up to £1000, to sell or even to catalogue vegetable varieties not on the National Lists or the EEC Common Catalogue. These regulations apply to all EEC countries, even though they are widely ignored. It is legal to grow them, and give seed to your neighbours, but they may not be sold.

Since 1973 we have been losing vegetable varieties by the hundred every six months. In June 1978 we lost 874 varieties, including the Pot Leek, traditionally grown by Durham miners on allotments fed with pit-pony manure; Market King tomatoes, the thin-skinned greenhouse favourite of the 1930s, and Victoria spinach, as British as Early Albert rhubarb. In addition we lost about 600 varieties that the Authorities regarded as 'synonyms', that is, too similar to be worth distinguishing. An example of this is the onion variety Up-to-Date, which the Ministry of Agriculture Department in charge of the National Lists considers identical with Bedfordshire Champion. Yet, according to the Ministry of Agriculture Bulletin No. 123 (Diseases of Vegetables), Up-to-Date has the greatest resistance to downy mildew, while Bedfordshire Champion has the least. Vegetables have qualities, like flavour, disease resistance and slowness to run to seed, of value to gardeners rather than to commercial growers, who want weight, a long shelf life, thick skins for long journeys to the supermarket, and bright colour to show through polythene prepacks.

The reason for these regulations is that horticultural and agricultural seeds can now be patented, earning large royalties, but to secure a patent they must satisfy the Ministry of Agriculture Department concerned (or its equivalent in any other EEC Country) that the variety is 'uniform, stable and distinct'. The smaller the National Lists are, the fewer varieties there are to search through and the less space in the catalogues need be given to those that gardeners have grown on their merits for up to a century.

These regulations have the backing of the multi-national companies who own most of the world's seed firms rather than of the remaining family firms, who still have to bow to commercial pressures but go on selling their old favourites as long as they can. They are being opposed in many countries by gardening organizations, and in May 1975 the Henry Doubleday Research Association (HDRA) began campaigning to save our heritage of vegetable varieties. These include not only our recent losses, but also those like the Martock bean, that has been grown in the Somerset village of Martock ever since the twelfth century by generations of homeseed savers. The HDRA runs a 'Seed Library', from which members can obtain their selections of seeds from the past for a fee to cover handling, postage and packing. These are grown by 'Seed Guardians' who take on the raising of a set of single kinds that will not cross, to be given away to their fellow members. Those who are interested should write to the Association at the address given in the Appendix on the work of this organic gardener's equivalent to the Royal Horticultural Society. A booklet entitled *Save Your Own Seeds* is available for those who wish to grow their own, saving not only scarce varieties, but also hard cash, for seeds, especially the latest varieties, are no longer cheap.

The varieties in this book have been chosen by a few famous seedsmen who consider that they have sufficient flavour, garden value and popularity to keep them in the catalogues for at least ten years, like Pilot, which has been a leading early pea since 1904 and is still selling. The regulations do not apply to species, so all herb seeds, salsify, scorzonera and other unusual vegetables can still be bought and sold. So can all bush and tree fruit.

Obtaining any choice of apples becomes increasingly hard now that we are rapidly becoming a two-apple nation – with only Cox and Bramley, apart from Golden Delicious and other sugared-water-tasting inports. The association keeps a record of the remaining craftsmen who still grow worthwhile collections of all fruit varieties, and will send the address of a stockist to anyone who sends a stamped, addressed envelope. It also runs a number of 'Vegetable Sanctuaries' in country houses open to the public, so that gardeners can see the treasures of the past and, in some cases, take part in tasting sessions. So long as the Englishman's and Englishwoman's home remains their castle, we have the right to grow what we choose in our own gardens, and to grow it how we like.

2.

Digging for a Diet

Everyone today is on a diet. Even the healthiest of us, happily eating just ordinary food, are 'dieted' by the food processors who have decided what it pays to make us eat by advertising, while inorganic farmers who use hormones and growth promoters can put additives even into simple steaks. The writing is on the packets and tins, but very small and no doubt legal until something happens and it has to be withdrawn. The only way to be sure of eating only what you choose to eat, is to buy it organically grown, or to grow it yourself, which is a great deal cheaper. Ask not at whom the fish finger points – it points at you!

It would be possible, but monotonous, to grow all your own food in your own garden, ideally supplemented by chickens and a goat. In practice we need to import our wheat for wholemeal bread, which is an ideal concentrated food with minerals and vitamins to digest it and make it the staff of a healthy life, but because we have taught birds to associate houses with food, it is not possible to grow wheat for home breadmaking in a small garden. As soon as it is ripe the birds will slaughter it, so buy your wheat from an organic farmer and grind it yourself to enjoy the full flavour of bread made from fresh milled flour. Or buy freshly ground flour from a food shop, for there is no reason why everyone should not enjoy home-baked bread. If you cannot tell the difference between real wholemeal and 'brown' give up smoking, for it is ruining your taste buds.

Organic and inorganic – the flavour difference

An even greater difference in flavour lies between organically grown and chemical-fed potatoes, and though these take up space in the garden, if possible grow all your own, even if you have to dig up the back lawn to do it. The potato is the gardener's best bargain in terms of food for space – about twice as much as the same area under wheat. Because it has the minerals and vitamins to digest its starches, these are not fattening, and it has a useful proportion of protein. Slimmers cut potatoes from their diet, because they would rather give up the tasteless and unattractive mush that is a poor-flavoured, high yielder like Pentland Crown, chemically fed, and eat biscuits instead. But a half-pound packet of starch-reduced slimming biscuits holds about as many carbohydrates as three pounds of potatoes, and without any vitamins to break them down. The pre-Potato Famine Irish were not fat, neither were the pre-Inca Peruvians, who also used potatoes as their staff of life.

The vitamins and minerals in vegetables

Because this book is concerned with gardening rather than nutrition these details are kept to a minimum. Table 2, however, shows why potatoes are always pushed in days of wartime rationing and why they are our most valuable vegetable.

Table 2: Comparative values of potato and other foods

	Moisture %	Carbohydrate %	Protein %
Biscuits (average)	10.0	66.10	Variable, but low
White bread	33.80	55.50	Variable, but small
Potatoes (boiled)	76.40	19.70	2.10
Artichokes (boiled)	79.60	16.90	1.60
Carrots (cooked)	87.00	9.30	1.20
Parsnips (cooked)	85.00	11.30	1.30
Turnips (cooked)	91.50	5.70	1.00

The potato has the highest dry matter, carbohydrate and protein of any root vegetable; organically grown potatoes, baked in their skins and eaten with butter, are a first-class meal for anyone. They are relatively shallow rooting, so cannot be as rich in minerals as the deep-driving salsify which wins on calcium, though they hold useful quantities of both iron and phosphorus (see Table 3). Sprouting broccoli and kale are far ahead on calcium. Though spinach is fantastically richer in calcium, phosphorus and iron, it holds so much oxalic acid that it locks both minerals up as oxalates, which pass from our bodies in urine. Other members of the same family contain less oxalic acid, and spinach in moderation is of value for the other nutrients it contains. Just as we rotate our crops so we should rotate our foods, and a diet of spinach alone could kill. An American once died from eating nothing but carrots.

Table 3: Mineral content of potato and other vegetables

	Calcium	Phosphorus	Iron	Copper
		Mg per 100g		
Potatoes (boiled)	4	33	0.46	0.15
Artichokes (boiled)	30	33	0.41	0.12
Beet (boiled)	30	36	0.70	0.14
Carrots (boiled)	46	38	0.60	0.11
Parsnips (boiled)	59	76	0.45	0.10
Radish (raw)	30	31	1.36	0.16
Salsify (boiled)	60	53	1.23	0.12
Turnips (boiled)	55	19	0.35	0.04
Broccoli (cooked)	160	54	1.52	–
Cabbage (cooked)	27	45	0.63	–
Lettuce (raw)	43	42	0.56	–
Spinach (cooked)	595	93	4.0	–

An average serving of vegetables is 100g, and this amount is used in all works on nutrition to calculate what every food supplies. There are a whole range of substances which lock up your vitamins and minerals. As an example, smoking uses up the body's Vitamin C, and folic acid, which is one of the Vitamin B group present in leafy vegetables (also in wheatgerm), in greater quantities raw than cooked, is made unavailable by antibiotics, the contraceptive pill, a high intake of alcohol or other refined carbohydrates, and tranquillizers like Valium. A shortage of folic acid in pregnancy can cause deformities at birth, especially spina bifida. Our bodies are made to absorb all vitamins and minerals that we need from our food, and in an age of additives this is best home-grown.

Table 4 shows that every vegetable has its strong points, with

Table 4: Vitamin content of potato and other vegetables

Vegetable	Vitamin C	Vitamin E	Niacin	Vitamin A IUs*	Thiamine	Riboflavin	Pyridoxine	Pantothenic Acid
		Mg per 100g				µg per 100g		
Potatoes (boiled)	10–14	0.10	1.20	20–40	100	40	320–650	220–320
Beet (boiled)	5	0.20	0.20	0–20	10	30	120	120
Carrots (boiled)	6	–	0.50	10,000	60	60	200	,120
Parsnips (boiled)	18	–	0.20	–	80	90	–	–
Turnips (boiled)	18	0.20	0.50	–	60	60	110	, 37
Radish (raw)	25	–	0.10	, 30	40	60	–	–
Lettuce (raw)	8	–	0.20	4,000	45	45	–	110
Cabbage (raw)	150	–	0.50	150	30	50	–	180
Cabbage (cooked)	80	–	0.30	80–170	?	?	?	?
Broccoli (cooked)	100	–	0.30	3,000–5,000	139	259	–	1,100
Spinach (raw)	18	–	0.20	6,790	60	45	–	110
Spinach (cooked)	13	–	0.20	3,445	?	?	?	?
Peas (raw)	25	–	2.10	–	400	200	79–100	1,040
Peas (canned)	?	?	?	?	110	60	–	120

* An International Unit (IU) of Vitamin A is 0.0006 mg of beta-carotene, which is converted into Vitamin A in the liver.

peas leading on thiamine, carrots on Vitamin A, with raw spinach a good second and lettuce, broccoli and cooked spinach following closely behind. Sprouting broccoli is best of all on pantothenic acid. Those who eat plenty of vegetables, of whatever kind, are getting a first-class mixture of vitamins and minerals, with sufficient fibre to make both bran and constipation totally unnecessary.

Gardening with allergies

The ordinary healthy family, growing what they like and eating it, have no need to worry about balancing their vitamins, but there are thousands of unfortunate people who suffer from allergies and other conditions that make dieting essential for medical reasons. It is hard for those who have not experienced the acute distress of sudden allergy symptoms to understand what a difference food can make, but still harder for those who have them.

When I was a boy I played chess with a friend's father, who began by taking his queen off the board to 'make a game of it', and finished up checkmating me with only a bishop and a knight. I am a coeliac, which means that I have diarrhoea and a high temperature if I have wheat, oats, rye or barley. No bread, no biscuits, no cake, no porridge, no beer (because of the barley), and above all no flour thickening in gravy or made-up foods. I can eat rice and maize, but for weeks I may do without them. Potatoes replace bread for me, and I manage on meat, eggs, fish, vegetables and fruit. If I were a vegetarian I should have 'lost my queen' because wholemeal bread is such an essential part of a vegetarian diet. Many coeliacs cannot take milk or dairy products, and many hay-fever sufferers, or those with constant colds or chest symptoms could well cut these out. Though this reduces calcium and riboflavin, all these can be obtained from vegetables, and it is simply a matter of eating (and growing) more of those that are high in what you are missing.

The Gluten-free Diet* (which I am on) is of considerable value to multiple-sclerosis cases, does not conflict with any medical treatments, and it costs less if you are able to grow your own vegetables, which replace the bought refined carbohydrate

*A copy of the Wholefood Gluten-free Diet is obtainable from The Henry Doubleday Research Association, Bocking, Braintree, Essex

foods you do not eat, including macaroni and semolina. The real problem comes for allergy sufferers.

Rotating diets

The most unfortunate are those who have multiple allergies, and have to try and make up a nutritionally balanced diet with the few foods they can eat safely, which is like playing chess with only a bishop and a knight. Frequently they are allergic to all grains, all pulses (pea-tribe seeds and vegetables), and all milk products. They dare not just concentrate on the foods they can eat, because they would then become allergic to these too, so they practise a five-day rotating diet, just as gardeners rotate their crops.

The aim is to have one meat, one fruit, one carbohydrate source and one leaf vegetable daily. Allergies run by natural orders as a rule, and just as more people are allergic to eggs than anything else, many sufferers are upset by the order *Solanaceae*, which means no tomatoes, no potatoes, no aubergines and no sweet peppers. If, however, you can safely eat one member of the family, then you can probably eat the others on the same day: carrots, parsnips and parsley all on your day for the *Umbelliferae*, or artichokes and lettuce when *Compositae* are on the menu. It is to help those whose health depends on picking the right vegetables that I have brought in the numbers on the tables. Table 5 gives an example of a rotating diet. Day Two's diet indicates the problem that arises because our fruits and vegetables come from so few natural orders. It is solved by the fact that there are many which belong to natural orders to which no one (as far as we know) has ever developed allergies, probably because we do not eat them often enough to start any. New Zealand Spinach in the *Aizoaceae*(1) has no relations and is available all the summer. Others in this useful class, but available almost all the year round are Lamb's-lettuce (13) and Miner's Lettuce (10) for salads. On Day Five, Salsify and Scorzonera could replace or join the artichokes and lettuce because all share membership of *Compositae* (3).

This rotation assumes that the maximum number of vegetables will be grown at home, but to add variety – or because the vegetables you have are out of season and your stores are exhausted – you can of course buy such exotics as sweet potato *(Convolvulaceae)* or yam *(Dioscoreaceae)*, which are excellent starchy vegetables often stocked where there is a West Indian

Table 5: A typical rotating diet

Day One	Day Two	Day Three	Day Four	Day Five
Beef	Fish	Lamb	Pork	Chicken
Carrots (12)	Potatoes (11)	Beet (2)	Turnip (4)	Artichokes (3)
Parsley (12)	N.Z. Spinach (1)	Chard (2)	Cabbage (4)	Lettuce (3)
Apples	Plums	Blackcurrants	Oranges	Raspberries

population. Bananas too are a source of carbohydrate, but their sweetness becomes a burden as the weeks go by. Sago from the sago palm and tapioca, made from the cassava root, are also non-home-grown additions that help out, but need Vitamin B complex which they lack entirely. Mint from the herb bed can also be brought in as a leaf vegetable. but this soon teaches us that herbs are not for eating in quantity. Parsley as an example is rich in iron, calcium and Vitamins A and C, but it contains apiol, an alkaloid once used to cause abortions, so eat it always in moderation.

Rotating diets are for extreme cases, and those who have allergy symptoms should first try giving up products that could contain additives. Carrots, as an example, can take up aldrin sprayed against carrot-fly, even from a field where it was last used ten years previously, and allergies work on tiny traces of substances that may affect only one person in a thousand, which can mean 56,000 sufferers in all Britain. There are plenty of best-selling books in this field, and many consultants, but do try growing more of the food you eat – the diet you dig is the safest of all.

3.

Food for the Soil

No organic gardener ever has enough compost material, for the sappy weeds of summer rot down to less than lawn-mowings and these make better compost mixed with something bulky and stemmy to add the celluloses, hemicelluloses and lignins that make lasting humus. One solution is to sow the common, striped, seeded sunflower, as sold by pet shops, a foot (30cm) apart each way in March or April on any spare ground (ideally where the septic-tank overflow escapes), and let them grow five feet (150cm) high, well before they produce flower buds. Then pull them and shake the soil off their roots for composting, and sow another batch, for the seed is cheap and lasts for about three years of sowings.

With enough room, it is a good idea to add a growing-square of compost material to the rotation, which in the country can be where you empty the results of bucket sanitation (even an Elsan bucket is safe for sunflowers), and two years growing sunflowers will 'tame' the most overfed soil, such as an old chicken-run site. If the chosen area is known to be full of clubroot spores, cut off the sunflowers above the first joint, so they shoot again and give a second cutting. The stumps die off in winter, ready for a second year's sowing, and you will not have moved spore-laden roots to your compost heap which may not get hot enough to kill them all in the bulk of soil. Sweetcorn is the crop that grows the most compost material as 'spin-off' from cobs to store in the freezer for the winter. Bash their stems with an axeback on a concrete path to speed rotting, which is cheaper and far quicker than any hand compost-chopper.

Cutting more compost material
Those who have transport, even a car with the back seats removed to take well-stuffed plastic sacks, can collect weeds. The rose-bay willow-herb, found on most waste land, is excellent and so are nettles, docks and cow-parsley, mown the previous day and left to wilt which allows much more to be stuffed into the bags and means hauling less water, so you make more finished compost to the trip. Bracken is the best bargain, for it holds 2.75 per cent potash (about the same as sunflowers) when cut fresh in summer, though only about 0.2 per cent when it dies and dries rusty-brown in autumn, for the potash is returned to store in the roots by then, and if it is cut in June or July and then again in September, it will be killed out in three years. Nettles, which offer three cuts – May, July and September, and docks are also destroyed by cutting, but always cut before they flower, so as to import no weed seeds into your garden and yet do the maximum damage to the weeds.

If you can cut quantities of cow-parsley and hemlock *(Conicum maculatum)* on waste ground or along roadsides near your garden in May and June, you will be destroying the food supply of the carrot-fly *(Psila rosea)*, the onion-fly *(Delia antiqua)* and the cabbage-root fly *(Delia brassicae)* which feed on the pollen and nectar of the order *Umbelliferae*, which is why you should not leave run-to-seed carrots in the rows. Weed-cutting does no harm ecologically, unlike spraying hedgerows with herbicides, and the gain in compost material and pest control is worth taking for free.

Building compost heaps
Bulk heaps are best built as cubes like hay stacks, and they should be started with a cross-shaped trench about six inches (15cm) deep and eight (20cm) wide, lined with rough wood kept in place with pegs to prevent the sides falling in. Cover the cross with brushwood or anything that will keep the material from filling it up, then pile on your material in a layer about a foot (30cm) thick in a six-foot (2m) square. On this, spread a layer, about an inch (25mm) thick, of any organic manure, ideally pigeon, poultry, rabbit or goat. Pigeon is by far the best and it is often free, for pigeon keepers know that it is 3.4 per cent

nitrogen and far too strong for garden use. But it is an excellent compost-heap 'activator' which is the source of nitrogen and phosphorus that the bacteria and fungi, which break down vegetable wastes to good humus and plant foods, must have to increase the heat of the heap to 180-190°F (65-70°C). This will cook the weed seeds like grains of rice, simmer convolvus roots like narrow potatoes and kill disease spores like a steam sterilizer.

Pile on another eight inches to a foot (20-30cm) thick layer and scatter on this enough garden lime to whiten the surface. The object of this is to prevent the heap becoming too acid as it will, especially if you can obtain lawn-mowings; and these can make up to half the bulk of the heap, provided they are spread through it and not left in one lump. Tennis clubs and sports grounds often have waste mowings to give away, and so long as as you do not use the grass until the second mowing after a selective weedkiller has been used, they are excellent. Add another layer of material, then more activator (which makes all the difference between compost and a rubbish heap), then more material, lime again and so on until your stack is as high as it will go, which is about five feet (150cm).

Slope in the sides a little, say to four feet (120cm) across the flat top of a heap, six feet (2m) at the base, so that it stays stable, with the open ends of the trenches extending about six inches (15cm) beyond the sides and ends. The object of these trenches is to let in plenty of air, for the bacteria that make compost need as much oxygen to produce the 180°F (65°C) temperature as if the heat had been produced by burning. Compost heaps have been described as 'bacterial bonfires', as they reduce the proportion of compounds containing carbon to those holding nitrogen from about 70-1 to between 10-1 and 14-1. This does not leave so much bacterial food that the bacterial increase in the soil robs the crops of available nitrogen and phosphorus, which is why we make compost rather than dig the rubbish straight in.

The carpet-covered compost heap
In addition to an activator and an air supply, compost needs moisture, and something to hold this and the heat in. The cheapest way to provide these is to obtain an old carpet from a second-hand shop or a skip, and cover the heap completely. A foam-backed carpet will last for several years, but the normal

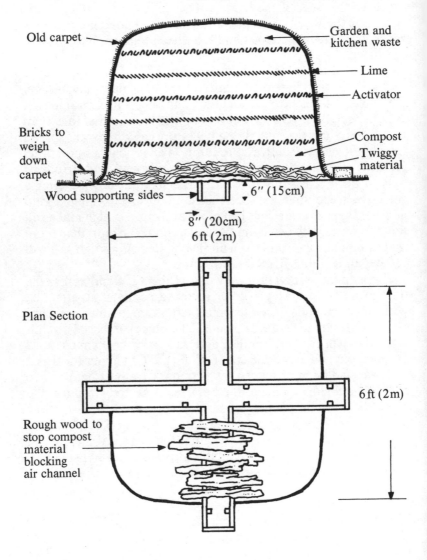

Section

Old carpet

Garden and kitchen waste

Lime

Activator

Bricks to weigh down carpet

Compost

Twiggy material

Wood supporting sides

6″ (15cm)

8″ (20cm)

6 ft (2m)

Plan Section

6 ft (2m)

Rough wood to stop compost material blocking air channel

1 Carpet-covered Compost Heap

type absorbs the moisture in the steam from the heap and rots down until it can itself go on the heap in about three years.

This kind of heap has the advantage that it can be made anywhere around the garden or rotated up and down its poorest portion so that all the drainings from it soak in and enrich the soil. If there is plenty of material make the heap longer, adding another cross trench every six feet (2m), but keeping the same height and width. If quantities of mowings are used, or there is difficulty in getting it to heat, set upright tomato or dahlia stakes along the trenches at two-foot (60cm) intervals and pull them out when it has been built, to leave extra upright air channels. A heap started in May should be ready to use by September, and can be tested by digging into it to see if the worms have moved in and it has become something like well-rotted manure with the plant remains showing but dark brown and easily broken. The temperature can be tested with a hot-bed therm-ometer, which should show a rapid rise to the required temper-ature in the first week, tapering off slowly until in three to four weeks it should be cold enough for the fungi to take over before the worms arrive.

The quality can be improved by turning the heap, but though this starts it heating again, it is hard work, and is unnecessary with carpet-covered heaps. Those just made in the open do not decay on the outsides which get too cold and dry, so must be turned to bring this unexpended portion of the soil's rations into the middle for consumption by the bacteria.

This system of composting is excellent with large quantities of material available at once, but most gardeners have to make their heaps little by little as compost material and kitchen waste accumulates. The original wooden New Zealand Box which stayed in one place and could last twenty years if it was well creosoted before it was nailed and bolted together can now cost almost as much as a garden shed.

Home-made wooden compost bins

Those who can find second-hand timber, or are determined to have a first-class traditional compost bin can make a standard, two-compartment model by following the diagrams and directions as given for the New Zealand Box in the HDRA leaflet *Give up Smoking Bonfires*, of which they have already given away about 600,000.

'A box with compartments 3ft (1m) square to hold 1 cubic

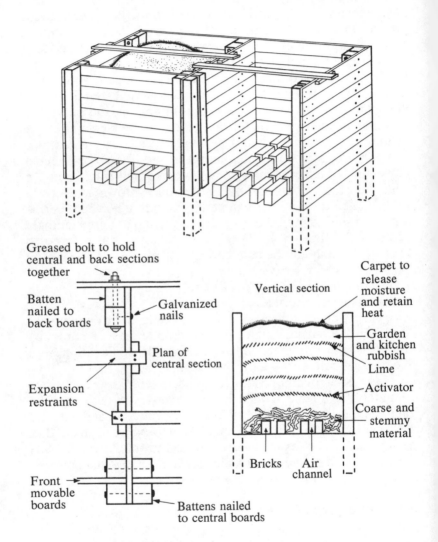

Greased bolt to hold central and back sections together

Batten nailed to back boards

Galvanized nails

Plan of central section

Expansion restraints

Front movable boards

Battens nailed to central boards

Vertical section

Carpet to release moisture and retain heat

Garden and kitchen rubbish

Lime

Activator

Coarse and stemmy material

Bricks

Air channel

2 New Zealand Box

yard (1 m³) of finished compost in each, takes 190ft (57m) of 4 x ½ in. (10 x 1 cm) sawn plank, six 4ft lengths of 2 x 2 in. (5 x 5 cm) timber and five 3ft (1m) lengths of 2 x 1½ in. (5 x 4cm) timber, but the dimensions are not important.

'Saw nine 6ft (2m) planks for the back and twenty-seven others 3ft (1m) long for the sides and middle. Then creosote everything, including the uprights, and leave to dry for about a week. Other wood preservatives such as Cuprinol or Solignum can be used, but all are more expensive than creosote. If you want to paint the bin green or black, use a bitumen paint (as sold for use on corrugated iron), because it will 'take' on top of creosote, which can then replace costly undercoat with a better rot preventer.

'Lay three of the 2 x 2 in. (5 x 5cm) uprights 3ft (1m) apart and nail the 6ft (2m) planks to the upper 3ft (1m) of the uprights. Then nail the 3ft (1m) planks at one end to the upper 3ft (1m) of the remaining three uprights. Dig six holes at the corners of the yard (metre) squares, fit the three uprights of the back into their respective holes but replace and firm the soil round the upright only at one end. Now put the lower foot (30cm) of the upright of the first end in its hole, and nail the free ends of the planks to the upright on the back, holding a brick against it to take the shock of the hammering. Then replace the soil round the upright and firm it well.

'When the middle and other end are fitted in this way, you have a strong, wooden letter 'E' in plan. Saw the remaining planks, which make up the removable board fronts of the compartments, into lengths of slightly less than 3ft (1m). Fit them into slots made by nailing the last five 3ft (1m) lengths of 2 x 1½ in. (5 x 4cm) sawn timber approximately ¾ in. (2cm) from the front uprights. You will need three to make the slots on both sides of the middle divider. Creosote the front boards and their sawn ends and let them dry before fitting.

'When you eventually need to move the heap, dig the soil out of the holes for the uprights as far as possible, then lift from both ends and replace in new holes dug ready 3ft (1m) apart on the new site. Do not try levering up the end with an iron bar, because this puts a great strain on the bin. Those who are better carpenters can nail the free ends of the 3 ft (1m) boards to a 3ft (1m) length of 2 x 1 in. (5 x 2.5cm) timber, which can be bolted to the upright with a ¼ in. (6mm) coach bolt 4 in. (10cm) long. Smear the bolts with motor grease or petroleum jelly before driving them through holes drilled in the uprights, the 2 x 1 in. (5 x 2.5 cm) wood and the planks from the inside, screwing the nuts on from outside, because they will be more likely to rust inside the heap. If well greased, they will screw off easily and the bin will come apart with less trouble. This is especially useful if you move house, as you can then pack your compost bin flat in the van.'

The essentials for success with this kind of heap are the air channels at the bottom (which can be trenches running from front to back of the same type used in the carpet-covered heap) and not attempting to save wood by leaving wide gaps between the planks, which lets air from the sides, destroying the draught (like holes in the sides of a chimney) and letting the heat and moisture out. There are many ready-made bins with wire sides which are utterly useless, serving only to dry the material till it is only fit to burn. Others are made of plastic and become flimsier and flimsier as they struggle to beat the carriage problems and go by post.

Bought compost containers
The best is the Rotol which is a black PVC cone with the top cut off and replaced with a lid 18 inches (45 cm) across, and about 3 feet (1 m) across the bottom. The sides are fluted and it works well because the moisture condenses and trickles down the flutings, which allows the centre to build up a good heat. It should be set on a smaller cross of air channels, which can be lined with bricks if these are available, and should be started with some rough, stemmy material to stop the air channels from blocking. Then it is charged by merely tipping in lawn-mowings, weeds and kitchen waste, with a scattering of lime at intervals and manure as an activator if you have it. Kitchen waste acts to some extent as an activator. A Rotol will swallow an incredible amount of rubbish and is ideal for a small garden to take daily contributions. It is simple, strong, relatively cheap and portable. When the contents cease to sink, lift it off, and remove the undecayed top of the cone of compost to start the next heap. The only drawback is that there will always be a quantity of tiny flies inside. These are vinegar flies and their tiny larvae help the breakdown, staying inside the Rotol and doing no harm to anyone.

With traditional wooden bins, rubbish is piled beside it to wilt and accumulate enough to cover the daily contribution

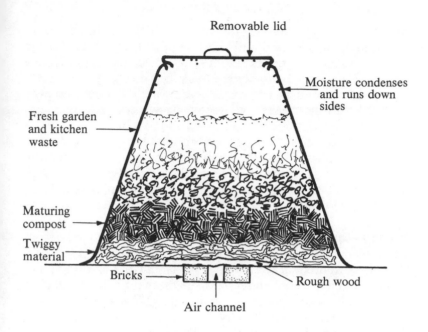

Removable lid

Moisture condenses and runs down sides

Fresh garden and kitchen waste

Maturing compost

Twiggy material

Bricks

Air channel

Rough wood

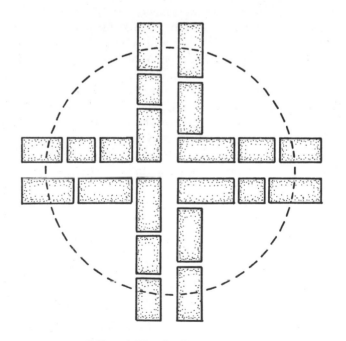

3 Rotol Plastic Compost Bin

from the kitchen, which should not include bones, meat scraps, or anything plastic, and only a minimum of wet paper. Layers can be thinner, 6-8 inches (16-20cm), and the process of filling continues until the heap ceases to sink. An essential is a loam pile beside the heap, where all grass weeds with soil-packed roots should be stacked to decay slowly for potting loam, because the commonest cause of failed compost heaps is leaving too much soil on the weed roots. Once soil layers used to be added, and soil used to cover the surface, but however well the soil is shaken off the weed roots, there will always be enough left to hold a full set of soil bacteria to organize high-temperature decay.

The Californian cylinder
The Californian cylinder, invented by Captain James Macdonald (US Navy Retired), a keen organic gardener working with a poor, dry soil, is made by obtaining short lengths of pig or sheep fencing, which is square-mesh, strong, wire netting. You need lengths 9-12 feet (3-4m) long and 3-4 feet (1m-1m 20) wide, so that they can be hooked together to make a cylinder about four feet (1m 20) in diameter. Make the usual cross of ventilation trenches and stand the cylinder on this, tying it to stout pegs driven well in because it has a considerable sail area and could blow over before it is fully made. Line it with opened-out cartons, sewn in place with a packing needle and twine. Then cover the channels with rough stemmy material as usual, and fill your cylinder with garden rubbish and kitchen waste.

The activator used by Captain Macdonald is what is tactfully called 'Household Liquid Activator' or 'Chairman Mao's Special', because it has been used successfully in China for more than forty centuries. This is human urine, in which adults produce 13.20g of nitrogen, 2.5g of potassium, 1.0g of phosphorus, 1.0g of sulphur and 5g of sodium every twenty-four hours. According to an organic gardening doctor, who experimented with the surplus samples from a hospital laboratory, there are no diseases likely to be passed on by urine in temperate climates (beware of Bilharzia in Africa) and the high salt level is not harmful in a compost heap, though it is enough to be appreciated by the whole beet family, which were originally seashore plants.

This useful free activator can be used for any compost heap, especially as an occasional tonic to speed up a slow-starting

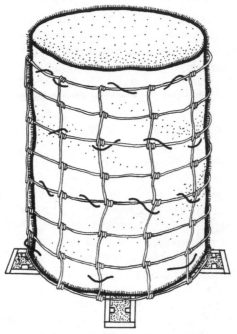

Sew carpet to pig fencing with string and packing needle

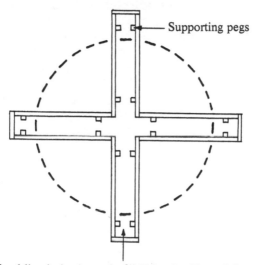

Supporting pegs

Wood-lined air channels 6″ (15 cm) wide and deep

4 Californian Cylinder Compost Bin

one, and as with every activator, the finished compost holds all the added minerals, which is why pigeon manure, which has 1.4 per cent phosphorus and 1.2 per cent potash as well as its generous nitrogen, is such a bargain. Four-foot (1 m20) square versions of the carpet-covered heap are excellent for small gardens, but they do have the trouble of taking the carpet off and putting it on again after every addition, so it is best to stack the material and pile it on every few days.

Good, well-rotted manure

Manure needs entirely different treatment, because its carbon–nitrogen ratio is about 20–1, even if it is strawy and fresh. The only good manure that gardeners can find today – now that farms have slurry tanks and tankers rather than yards and dung-carts – is from riding stables or individual horse owners who have used straw litter. Peat is second best, but shavings litter manure is useless, because the carbon–nitrogen ratio of shavings is 500–1 and the damage it can do to a soil lasts for years.

To convert raw manure from a stable to well-rotted 'real good stuff' in four to six weeks, build a heap about four feet (1 m20) wide and high, tapered into about thirty inches (75 cm) across the top, and as long as the load needs, and whack it firm with the flat of the spade. It is best built on a sheet of 500-gauge polythene, to collect the drainings which would otherwise be wasted, folded up at the sides and ends and held up with stakes. Then cover it with a second sheet, weighed down all round with heavy wood or stones to stop the wind tearing it away. The best polythene for this purpose is discarded from commercial growers' polythene tunnels, because it is free and semi-opaque from the action of sunlight (which is why it is discarded).

The steam from the heating fresh manure condenses on the underside of the sheet, especially at night, and prevents further heating, while lack of air stops continued breakdown. This is the reverse of composting, for the object is to take the straw a stage or two further along the road to humus, to 'tame' the fierce fresh nitrogen and to preserve the plant foods until they are needed, by a process more like silage-making than composting. The system removes the risk of 'firefang' fungus which invades manure heaps with a white mycelium that wastes both nitrogen and humus. In the past the heap would be spread, watered with brine and restacked, but the polythene system saves us this trouble.

Dealers are often keen to sell pig manure, because farmers know that the copper sulphate they mix in the feed for faster fattening will build up to toxic levels in the soil and stay there. Organic farmers who do not use copper or other additives never sell their manure. They value their fertility, so it is only the inorganic who sell manure and buy chemicals instead. Manure from cows is safe but sloppy, even with straw, and it pays to buy baled straw and add an extra 20 per cent to increase the humus, unless they have been generously littered. The polythene process will convert it all to better manure than you can ever buy.

Autumn leaf humus
Dead leaves are the most wasted source of lasting humus today, and in most towns and suburbs it is possible to obtain an extra supply, either unofficially by bribing the roadmen, or officially through the council. Ratepayers are entitled to have the benefit of the leaves that their rates have paid to be swept, instead of paying to have them burnt, releasing dangerous air pollution. Write to your local paper and make a row, for five cubic yards (or metres) of leaves as swept, stack to three, and rot to two, which is roughly a ton. This is rather richer in plant foods than peat and far cheaper, even if the roadmen in your area are greedy, and its help in holding moisture on sandy soils and lightening heavy clays goes on for years.

A traditional leaf-mould heap can go in dry shade under trees where nothing much will grow. Level the ground and drive in stout posts three feet (1 m) high at the corners, adding extra posts every yard (metre) if you are going to have leaves enough to make a large heap. Staple three-feet (1 m) high wire netting to the outsides of the posts and pile in the leaves as they are gathered, removing dead branches and paper litter if they are swept from the streets. Hose the heap once or twice the first summer, especially if this is a dry one.

Never include weeds or garden rubbish in the leaf pile (or dead leaves in a compost heap), for the decay of leaves is carried out by fungi that need no oxygen because there is very little heating, and the whole process is much slower. After a year the heap will have sunk and firmed, so the posts can be dug up with the netting and moved to make the enclosure for next autumn's leaves. Year old leaf-mould is good enough to dig into a sandy soil or to lighten clays, but for potting soil it should wait for another year.

Hastened leaf-mould heaps

There is a legend that plane and chestnut leaves are 'poisonous' and will not decay, though if this was true there would be seams of coal-like unrotted leaves built up through the centuries of chestnut coppices that grow the hop poles of Kent. They merely need more time, and there are two ways round the problem. Start with a nine-foot or three-metre length on metre-wide wire netting and hook the ends together as though making a Californian Cylinder. There is no need to dig air channels, because no oxygen is needed; just staple it upright to a stout post, fill it with well-trodden leaves, and pour Household Liquid Activator on them. This will break down refractory leaves in one year rather than three, and produces improved decay for leaves of any kind. This should really be called a 'Peggy Pile' after Dr Peggy Ellis of the HDRA, the inventor of the method.

Another system begins with a traditional leaf stack, but in the spring, as soon as ample lawn-mowings are available, turn the leaf stack, mixing in about 25 per cent of its bulk of the mowings. This distributes the mowings among the leaves, where they decay with the help of the leaf-mould-making fungi, which are evidently delighted with their new diet, for again they will produce good leaf-mould in as little as six months. This is neither leaf-mould nor compost, free from weed seeds because there should be none in spring mowings, and none among the leaves, making an excellent surface coat to go between bush fruit, or as a mulch for no-digging gardeners.

Leaf humus without heaps

The head gardeners of the past valued leaf-mould for its lasting qualities, and when they had to *buy* it insisted on oak or beech because this had its plant foods the most firmly locked up by tannins. Otherwise they used leaf-mould made from every leaf on the estate, for peat has been used for barely fifty years as an ingredient for every potting soil. Because it has so little rapidly rottable carbohydrates, dead leaves do not rob the soil of nitrogen and phosphorus, so those who have a new garden full of raw subsoil can spread raw, dead leaves even six inches (15 cm) thick on the surface and have them spread through the top eight inches (20 cm) or sow with a powerful Rotavator, which chops them and distributes them through the surface layer. Give two cultivations, and before the second one spread as much as a pound a square yard (500g a square metre) of lime to correct acidity. The cost of hiring the machine and operator will be far less than having any gardener dig in the leaves, and it will add *enough* humus material to make a real difference.

Municipal fertility

Dried sewage sludge is so scarce since OPEC put up the cost of the fuel oil for drying, that there are only two sources. These are the Mogden Sewage Treatment Works, Isleworth, Middlesex, and the Yorkshire Water Organics, Mitchel Laithes, Clough Lane, Earlisheaton, Dewsbury, West Yorkshire. Both authorities will deliver, for a charge that varies with distance, and both supply this dark grey, odourless powder ready bagged for those who can fetch it and save the carriage. Its comparison with farmyard manure is shown in Table 6.

Table 6: Comparison between dried sewage sludge and farmyard manure

	Morganic Middlesex %	Dewmus Yorkshire %	Farmyard manure %
Moisture	10.0	13.0	77.0
Ash-free dry matter	50.0	40.3	17.0
Nitrogen	3.0	2.5	0.6
Phosphorus	2.3	2.5	0.3
Potassium	0.2	0.46	0.2

In terms of organic matter and plant foods for weight carried in the back of the car, both sludges beat farmyard manure, and as compost-heap activators and food for lawns, they are ideal. Both contain lead and cadmium (and there has been a panic on the dangers of both substances, but these two sludges meet the Ministry of Agriculture safety standards). As it is likely that the campaign against lead in petrol will give us leadless motoring, so no more tiny particles of tetraethyl lead will wash off the streets into the sewers, the risk will end. There is now a process that will take the cadmium out of industrial effluents, and show a profit on the recycled metal, so this pollution will end too as soon as local authorities can force industry to use this electrical method of extraction.

The uses of dried sludge

The cost of drying is unlikely to fall, but dried sludge, as distinct from the liquid which is spread on farms by the tanker load, will still be a garden bargain for two special uses which do not involve any risk from toxic metals. It is an excellent compost activator, mixed with 25 per cent of seaweed meal. Keep it near the heap in a watertight container, to scatter at the rate of 4 oz a square yard (1 10g a square metre) of heap surface after every layer, because it contains enough lime, including that in the seaweed, to keep the heap from becoming too acid. Lime can be used with dried sludge without any complications for heaps with a high proportion of lawn-mowings.

The other use is as a lawn food for, to organic gardeners, the lawn is a source of compost or mulching material as well as somewhere to sit, and a green background to brilliant borders. All lawns appreciate 8 oz a square yard (220g a square metre) of dried sludge in March or April, as a general food, but on weedy lawns, especially with sandy soils, mix 10 parts of the sludge by weight with 7 parts of sulphate of ammonia and 3 of sulphate of iron. Sulphate of ammonia is a chemical fertiliser and it is here employed to poison not only daisies but clover, which increases the risk of slipping on sports turf, particularly on tennis courts. Scatter this at the rate of 4-6 oz a square yard (110-160g a square metre) in spring.

Organic lawn care

Organic gardeners do not regard clover as a weed, for it is fixing useful nitrogen, and as long as a lawn is green and highly productive they are content. Cutting out the sulphate of ammonia, and using only the sulphate of iron controls fairy-ring fungus and moss. Often this is a lawn's protest against having mowings taken off once a fortnight, and nothing given back, so feeding with dried sludge at the same rate again at midsummer will build up a failing lawn.

On a heavy clay the lawn sand recipes can be made up with dry sand rather than sludge. A standard old-fashioned lawnsand is a good daisy killer and is more effective against pearlwort than modern killers. Rosette weeds, like flat thistle or dandelions, can be killed individually by putting a level teaspoonful (5 ml) of salt on their crowns. The salt (which can be the cheapest obtainable, not good, sea salt as sold in health-food shops) does no harm to the grass; in fact it rather favours the finer grasses.

Those who do not mind clover can cure moss by spreading 4 oz a square yard (110g a square metre) of slaked lime in June.

Well-rotted leaf-mould spread on lawns in the autumn will be taken under by earthworms and slowly builds up humus at grass-roots level. Tea leaves, obtained in quantity from a café, are excellent brushed into the lawns, for they are 'bite-sized' for worms and contain about half as much nitrogen as dried blood locked up by more tannins than there are even in oak leaves. They are splendid as a six-inch (15cm) layer in the bottom of fruit-tree planting holes, to supply slow-released nitrogen when the roots get down to them. Leaving a stout, plastic bag at a café will accumulate a really concentrated compost material that provides lasting long-term humus that is real value for the cost of the petrol to fetch it.

Lime, the soil sweetener
The best lime for everyone is ordinary garden lime, because though ground limestone, which is calcium carbonate, lasts longer in the soil, it is used by farmers, and therefore hard to buy in small quantities. Garden, or 'slaked', lime is very fine grains of calcium hydroxide which act quickly, for example in lowering the acidity of a compost heap to help the bacteria that produce rapid heating. Because there is so much carbonic acid excreted by the roots of all plants and weeds, it becomes calcium carbonate by a chemical reaction in the soil, while compost-heap bacteria are also producing carbonic acid in quantity, so there is no problem.

Minerals that matter
Ground dolomite limestone, which is half calcium carbonate and half magnesium carbonate, is used instead of lime at about 8 oz a square yard (220g a square metre), for tomato borders or anywhere that a previous gardener has used quantities of potash fertilizers. These fertilizers lock up magnesium, making the lower leaves of tomato plants turn yellow while the veins stay green, a condition also seen in raspberries and other crops, and usually mistaken for a virus instead of the consequence of too many chemicals. One dressing is usually enough, though inorganic gardeners who still go on piling on the potassium would need it every other year. It can be obtained from the Henry Doubleday Research Association if you fail to find it locally.

So can rock potash, or Adularian shale, mined in Scotland, which is 8-10 per cent potassium, far more readily available than in the basalt, feldspar, and granite used in Europe. It lasts in the soil without washing out like chemical fertilizers and is ideal for the gardener who wants to grow gooseberries on a poor sandy soil. Clays usually have enough potassium, waiting for the roots to pick out, but rock potash at about 8 oz a square yard (220g a square metre) is an organic answer for all potash-hungry crops, especially potatoes.

The accepted division between organic fertilizers and the mineral sources that can be used where a soil is short of an essential plant food is to allow fine-ground, natural rock particles which are what roots normally find in the soil, or which soil bacteria or fungi can make available to them. A soluble chemical fertilizer, like nitrate of soda, muriate and sulphate of potash and superphosphate washes from the soil and is taken up directly by the plant, with a number of consequences to flavour and pest and disease resistance. A classic example is Kainite, from the dried-up sea-salt at Stassfurt in Germany, which is a mixture of potassium, magnesium and sodium chlorides, used for sugar beet by inorganic farmers in Britain, and regarded as 'organic' in Europe, because it is not 'refined' but used as it is dug. In Israel they have the Dead Sea, with much the same mixture of salts, but these are sorted out and the potassium chloride is sold separately. Potatoes, unlike people, do not consider a chemical organic if it comes from Germany, and inorganic if from Israel, and grow with that undesirable 'inorganic' flavour that every organic gardener knows when he runs out of home-grown and has to buy from a greengrocer.

Wood ashes

Wood ashes are used by most organic gardeners, but the potash here, which is mainly potassium carbonate, washes out just as badly as chemical sources from the sandy soils that need it. They vary widely from 37 per cent potash for lime-tree branch ashes to 8 per cent for oak and birch, but they are also rich in calcium, with spruce up to 60 per cent and elm down to 17 per cent, so their best use is scattered, in place of lime, on compost-material layers, where there will be some complex chemical reactions, one of which produced the saltpetre (potassium nitrate) that made the first gunpowder for the Chinese in 350 BC. Do not try to use up the ashes from a wood-burning stove with extra thick layers in the compost heap, or you will unbalance it chemically. Spread your ashes on the floor of the poultry house under the perches, and they will dry out the droppings until these can be swept rather than scraped out, with a real saving in trouble, time and smell. There is a chemical reaction between the alkaline potassium carbonate, and the acid ammonium carbonate of the poultry manure, and the result is as shown in Table 7. The potassium is converted to a less readily available form, and the result is a far better balanced manure than anything else from the poultry shed. Keep the grey-brown powder in a dry place, and use it as a good general organic fertilizer at the rate of 4-8 oz a square yard (110-220g a square metre). It is worth keeping chickens, if you have a wood stove, to get the fertilizer.

Table 7: Poultry manure, before and after mixing with wood ash

	Fresh droppings %	Wood ash treated %
Moisture	72.00	16.70
Organic matter	20.00	89.85
Nitrogen	1.66	0.90
Phosphorus	0.91	1.50
Potash	0.48	2.12

Organic fertilizers

Though there is a slowly released source of phosphorus in rock phosphate, which is fossilized dead fish from dried-up seabeds mainly in North Africa, and Gafsa rock phosphate is bought in quantities by organic farmers, no gardeners have any need to use it, because fine bonemeal is easy to buy and offers both phosphorus and nitrogen. There are a number of organic fertilizers of this type which are relatively expensive, including dried blood, which provides the tonic effect of quickly released nitrogen, for a crop that has hung about too long; hoof and horn meal, offering slowly released nitrogen; and blood, fish and bonemeal, which is, today, material from slaughter houses and fish-finger factories, that cannot go into cattle cake. The quantities to use will be quoted in the month-by-month chapters, but gardeners really need them less often than they may think they do. Table 8 gives details of the chemical comparison between these fertilizers.

Table 8: Average analysis of organic fertilizers

	Moisture %	Nitrogen %	Phosphorus %	Potash %
Dried blood	–	9-13	0.8	–
Hoof and horn meal	–	6.5-13.2	0.1-0.2	–
Bonemeal	0.2-14	0.3-4.6	14.1-33.2	1–1
Bone and meatmeal	6.0	3.9-12.3	0.9-19.0	1–1
Fish meal	–	6.3-8.9	6.0-8.9	1–1
Seaweed meal	–	2.80	0.22	2.29

Seaweed is an excellent tomato fertilizer as it holds more potash than phosphorus. There are many liquid seaweed preparations for use as 'foliar feeds', for plants feed not only through their roots, but their leaves as well. This was discovered during World War II, when our blockade prevented the French importing copper sulphate for spraying their vines, so they used copper nitrate instead, and discovered they were curing the symptoms of nitrogen deficiency.

Seaweed contains an almost complete set of trace elements, including boron, bromine, calcium, copper, iodine, magnesium, manganese and sodium, all in forms that leaves can take in readily. All plants, but especially trees, throw away unwanted minerals through their leaves, and take what they want as it goes by, so if the leaves of any crop are strangely discoloured, or trees show the colours of autumn at the wrong season, try using seaweed sprays on the leaves. You will not know what the shortage was, but this does not matter – if the trouble has stopped that is good enough.

Soil testing

A soil-testing outfit is of little value to an organic gardener, because it merely counts the loose change in the pockets of his garden, and ignores its investments and bank account. The reliable test is for lime, and this apparatus consists of a kind of liquid litmus paper which is poured into a small china scoop with a sample of soil, and a colour chart that shows the pH level and how much lime is needed to bring it to between pH 6.5 and pH 7.0 which is neutral and the level at which most garden vegetables and fruit will thrive.

The shortage all sandy soils may have is potassium, because heavy liming and dressings of phosphorus can lock the potash out of root reach on clays, and on sands, chemical potash salts wash away. Gooseberries show potassium deficiency when the leaves turn a rather blue-green colour, have light-brown bands round the edges and fall early; tomatoes also have light-brown scorching at the leaf edges, and the fruit ripens patchily, with green and yellow areas merging into red, instead of changing from green to red shade by shade, while potato leaves turn bronzy green with brown spots between the veins and foliage dying down too soon for a good crop. Broad, french and runner beans show light-brown leaf-edge scorching, as do beet, cabbage and lettuce.

The cure for what is usually taken to be some deadly virus or new disease is rock potash, which can be scattered between the growing plants, for unlike a chemical fertilizer it will not scorch the foliage and takes time to act. Fork the powder lightly in during the summer and there should be no trouble the following year. Wood ashes can be used for quick action, but remember that they vary. Twigs have most and apple prunings burn to make an ash worth saving for emergencies.

Comfrey for fertility
The best source of quickly available potassium for organic gardeners is comfrey, and everyone should have a comfrey bed to supply a very useful high-potash liquid manure, for tomatoes setting their first fruit and other potash-hungry plants. This powerful, long-lived perennial, which is also a good food, a fodder crop and a valuable medicinal herb, needs a position in full sun away from trees or privet hedges, so its roots can go down deeply to gather minerals far out of reach of most garden plants.

Comfrey rarely sets seed and is grown from offsets, which are short sections of root each with a growing point which should be just below the surface when they are planted two feet (60cm) apart each way at any time of year except between November and the end of January, when the roots are entirely dormant and there may be losses in hard weather. Otherwise comfrey is fully hardy. It is a natural hybrid which took place in Upland, Sweden, between *Symphytum officinale,* the herbalist's comfrey, and *S. asperum,* the blue-flowered prickly comfrey from Russia, so the modern mixtures are correctly called *S. uplandicum.*

They were sorted out at the HDRA Trial Ground at Bocking,

and the usual garden varieties are Bocking 14, with thin stems and mauve flowers, which will grow three feet (1 m) high if left uncut, and is the highest in potash, and Bocking 4, which has thick, solid stems, large leaves, and flowers nearer to violet in colour. This has a higher yield, starts growing rather later in the spring, and is grown in many countries as stock feed. Its leaves are used as a green vegetable, but they are not particularly attractive, and the major uses of the plant today are as a source of liquid manure and as a dried herbal tea mainly used to alleviate arthritis.

Starting and keeping comfrey

The essential first step to starting a comfrey bed is to search out all the roots of perennial weeds, for it is a permanent garden feature like an asparagus bed, but much more lasting. Dig in manure to give it a start, and after planting hoe between the rows to kill out annual weeds and especially grass. The best planting times are March, April and May, or in September, which gives them time to become well established before winter. Summer plantings do well if they are watered well after planting and during the week that follows.

Spring-planted comfrey should be cut with shears about two inches (5 cm) above the ground in July or August, to prevent it flowering the first season, and this provides enough foliage for a trial of its qualities as a liquid manure. Leave further growth to die down in the plant in October and build up strength for a full cutting programme the following year. This begins with a first cut in April and the last in late September or early October, roughly every six weeks, which means four or five cuts a year.

After a comfrey bed has been planted for two years, it can be increased very simply by driving a spade through these established plants about three inches (8 cm) below the surface in March when the growing points are just showing. Lift off the crowns of the plants and cut them up into sections of root, each with a growing point, to replant where required. Do the cutting up over a spread newspaper (for though comfrey rarely seeds, every fragment of root will grow), fold up the paper and dump it in the dustbin. A weed is a plant in the wrong place and carelessly scattered comfrey can be an awkward weed.

If you are extending the comfrey bed, fill in the holes with soil, and wait for the decapitated plants to grow again, missing two cuts but becoming rather more productive next season. If, however, you planted them in what you now feel is the wrong place, spread about a quarter of an ounce (7g) of ammonium sulphate (the safest known weedkiller) on the cut surface of the roots left in the ground. This will destroy them completely, and in about four weeks the chemical becomes sulphate of ammonia, which is a common chemical fertilizer and washes harmlessly from the soil. It can be used to kill swarms of small comfrey plants where a Rotavator has been used in an attempt to kill comfrey, or where it has been dug out, leaving the soil full of fragments. Stir 1 lb (450g) of the white crystals into a gallon (4.5 litres) of water and apply with a rosed can over a ten-foot (3m) square area. In eight weeks any crop can be sown or planted after it.

This total weedkiller can be used to destroy horseradish and other awkward weeds, but it is comparatively expensive, and no organic gardener likes using chemicals. This substance is, roughly speaking, sulphate of ammonia made crooked, and the greedier a weed is for nitrogen the more it takes, which is why it should only be used when weeds are growing strongly, never in autumn or winter. It kills not by poison but by bad diet – like killing rats by feeding them only white bread and white sugar. In eight weeks you can plant or sow any crop on the treated area. It is never poisonous to birds or pets, and it produces an *increase* in the worm population after use.

When the plants die down completely, dig between the rows to take out any perennial weeds, and lime if necessary. Once a comfrey bed is established and growing well, there is little need to hoe because the foliage meets in a solid mass, suppressing annual weeds. Because it is producing more than a hundredweight (50.80kg) of foliage a season, comfrey needs generous feeding. Always give it manure on the surface in spring – ideally deep-litter poultry manure, with straw or peat litter – spread as a two-inch (5cm) thick surface coat; pigeon manure is excellent and so is sewage sludge. Because it is not a legume (it belongs to the *Boraginaceae*, the anchusa or forget-me-not family) and has no bacterial helpers fixing the nitrogen that gives it remarkably high protein, it needs plenty of manure, but can take it very crude. Fresh poultry manure or household liquid activator which you cannot use direct on other crops will keep it growing to produce a very much better organic fertilizer than the manure you give it.

The garden uses of comfrey

It has a carbon-nitrogen ratio of 9.8–1, so it is a kind of 'instant compost'; when wilted overnight to concentrate it, and spread along the bottom of maincrop potato trenches at the rate of 1½ lb a foot (2kg a metre) of row in place of lawn-mowings, it lowers the potato-scab rate as well as producing excellent crops of first-class flavour, because of its very high level of immediately available organic potash. Table 9 shows the comparative analysis of wilted comfrey, compost and farmyard manure.

Table 9: Comparative analysis of wilted comfrey, Indore compost and farmyard manure

Material	Water %	Nitrogen (N) %	Phosphorus (P_2O_5) %	Potash (K_2O) %	Carbon-Nitrogen ratio
Farmyard manure	76.0	0.64	0.23	0.32	14:1
Russian comfrey (wilted)	75.0	0.74	0.24	1.19	9.8:1
Indore compost	76.0	0.50	0.27	0.81	10:1

The analysis figures given in Table 10 for dried comfrey show why Bocking 14 is the favourite for fertility with about a third more potash than Bocking 4, making it rather bitter to eat as a vegetable and unattractive to rabbits, while the wild *S. officinale* has the least of all. The carpeting comfrey *S. grandiflorum*, with its larger, white, bell flowers hanging from short, thin stems in May, contains little potassium, and no allantoin, the medicinal principle which has earned comfrey the names of 'knitbone' and 'wound heal' in all the languages of Europe.

Table 10: Comparative analysis of dried comfrey, Bocking 4 and Bocking 14

	Bocking 4 %	Bocking 14 %	*S. officinale* %
Calcium	2.35	2.77	1.31
Phosphoric acid	1.25	0.75	0.72
Potassium	5.04	7.09	3.09
Iron	0.253	0.144	0.098
Manganese p.p.m.	137	133	85
Cobalt	trace	trace	–

The problem of using comfrey in potato trenches is that in cold springs there may not be enough bulk grown in time for earlies. It is, however, better to leave potatoes chitting rather longer in a cold season so they wait for the comfrey, and to lay the long, sprouted seed tubers flat on the surface of the wilted comfrey, which heats a little and warms them ahead.

Comfrey's most popular use today is as a liquid manure. This is made in two ways. The first is to put 14 lb (6 kg) of freshly cut comfrey in a twenty-gallon (90 litre) fibreglass waterbutt (metal drums rust and add toxic quantities of iron oxide to the liquid manure), fill up with rain or tap water, replace the lid to exclude the light, and in about four weeks a clear liquid can be drawn from the tap at the bottom. A comparison between this and commercial liquid feeds made up according to the manufacturer's directions is given in Table 11. Tomorite is a popular inorganic tomato feed, and Marinure an organic one based on seaweed.

Table 11: Comparative analysis of comfrey and two commercial liquid feeds

	Tomorite %	Marinure %	Comfrey %
Dry matter	0.1410	0.0480	0.4090
Nitrogen	0.0130	0.0070	0.0140
Potash	0.0139	0.0019	0.0340
Phosphorus	0.0093	0.0001	0.0059

The comfrey liquid has three times as much potassium, a third less phosphorus and rather more nitrogen than the other two, which is why it is ideal for tomatoes, onions, gooseberries, beans and all potash-demanding crops. Because the liquid is clear it can also be used as a foliar feed, and will not block a watering-can rose when it is applied generously as a tonic.

The disadvantage of this system is that comfrey foliage is about 3.4 per cent protein, and when proteins break down they smell. The answer is to use a plastic cask or a metal drum, well coated with black bitumen paint inside and out, and bore a hole in the side just above the bottom. Stand the container on bricks or stout wood so it is high enough off the ground to allow a dish to go under it. Fill the container with cut comfrey, packing it solid and putting something heavy like a lump of concrete on the surface. In about three weeks, a black liquid will drip from the hole into the dish to collect and dilute with 4 fluid oz of the concentrate to the gallon of water (1 part concentrate to 40 parts water). The concentrate can be stored in a screwtop bottle if you do not want to use it immediately. The analysis averages:

Nitrogen (N)   0.11 per cent
Phosphorus (P)   0.06 per cent
Potassium (K)   0.55 per cent

If this mixture is to be used as a foliar feed, it should be filtered through a pair of old tights, because it will contain fine particles that may block the syringe. The residue of comfrey left in the bottom of the container when the black liquid ceases to drip is good compost and can be tipped out and dug in before the container is refilled for another charge. The process can be hastened by pouring some urine in to give a high nitrogen start and some extra potassium.

Comfrey foliage holds far more carbohydrate and protein than fibre, which is why it is a good pig food but a poor compost material. It can be used to add more plant foods, and even as an activator, but it rots down to very little compared with high-fibre material such as sunflower stems. So use the surplus mixed in with other material. The liquid-manure methods waste less of the nitrogen. It is of greater value as a surface coat, spread between tomato plants or under soft fruit, especially gooseberries. Here it can be covered with lawn-mowings (which should not be in contact with the stems of the mulched crop), which will speed its decay into a kind of surface-made compost, from which plant foods will wash down into the soil below.

Making comfrey tea
Though comfrey leaves can be used direct to make tea in summer, it is more convenient to dry them for use round the year. Pick the largest mature leaves you can find, and lay them on small-mesh wire-netting in the sun, so they have free circulation of air below them as well as above. When they are floppy and drying at the edges, finish them off in an electric oven turned low and with the door open to let out the steam. Crush them when crisp and store in a screwtop jar. Comfrey tea is usually mixed with equal parts of ordinary tea and about six cups a day has kept away the pain of arthritis for thousands of people who are convinced that it is the finest medicinal herb of all.

4.

January

January is the month without outdoor sowing or planting, when food depends on stored roots, what is frozen or bottled and what can still be dug or picked in the garden. Salads that can be cut quickly even under cleared snow are lamb's-lettuce, miner's lettuce and landcress, with Winter Density the hardiest cos variety sometimes still available from the earlier sowings that have survived from the batch for autumn eating. Raw cabbage is the quickest winter salad, because you can clear one of the white domes that are savoys or January Kings, cut through the stem and get back into the warm with perhaps 3 lb (1.3 kg) of nutritional value, that soars in shop price in hard weather.

Those who have allergies will see that there is still a wide range of the numbers that abbreviate the natural orders that they can eat each day, and also at what date they could have sown to have had them ready for eating in this dead centre month before the gardener's year starts turning again.

The leaf beets, chard and spinach beet, winter spinach and a full range of the cabbage family are ready to gather when weather permits, and the large leaves of chard can be twisted (not cut) off far more quickly than picking spinach. Never strip a single plant but take leaves in turn so that there are enough to protect the new leaves that will be ready later. It pays to pack the garden with every possible winter vegetable, to allow for losses and to give recovery time from crops that produce well into the spring. The value of wide spacing shows in winter, for leaf

Available for eating	Family	Sowing	Planting
Artichokes, Jerusalem	3	–	February-March
Beans (dried or frozen)	7	May-June	–
Beet (leaf)	2	April	–
Beet (stored)	2	May	–
Broccoli (heading)	4	May	July
Brussels sprouts	4	May	June-July
Cabbage	4	June	July
Carrots (stored)	12	May	–
Celeriac	12	March	May
Celery	12	March-April	May-June
Hamburg parsley	12	March-April	–
Kale	4	April	June-July
Lamb's-lettuce	13	July-August	–
Landcress	4	August-September	–
Leeks	8	April	July
Lettuce	3	March-July	–
Miner's lettuce	10	July-August	–
Onions (stored)	8	March	–
Parsnips	12	February-March	–
Peas (dried or frozen)	7	January-May	–
Potatoes (stored)	11	–	April-May
Pumpkins	5	April	May
Radish, Chinese	4	July	–
Salsify	3	March-April	–
Scorzonera	3	March-April	–
Spinach (winter)	2	September	–
Swedes (stored)	4	July	–
Sweetcorn (frozen)	6	April-May	–
Tomatoes (bottled)	11	–	May-June
Turnips (stored)	4	June-July	–

vegetables in contact with each other provide more shelter for slugs and hold moisture that leads to rotting.

January is seed catalogue time, and though seed potatoes and all bush or tree fruit should have been ordered early in the autumn to give a choice of varieties, it pays to place one sizeable seed order with a good firm, to secure the essentials and save on postage – there is always a surcharge on small orders, which makes afterthoughts expensive. The following varieties are likely to be available for several years to come, and are kinds with flavour of real garden merit. They may well be replaced by better varieties in the future, but it is also possible that their successors will be vegetable equivalents to tasteless Golden Delicious apples, and certain that they will be more expensive.

Vegetables of value

Broad Beans
The Sutton: A foot high (30cm) to sow a foot (30cm) apart each way for succession from March to July.

Aquadulce Claudia: The best for November sowing to dodge blackfly. A very hardy, long-pod variety.

Hylon: A new, heavy-cropping long pod, with 10-11 seeds a pod, for autumn or spring sowing. Holds its flavour well frozen.

Unrivalled Green Windsor: Five large seeds to a pod. Sow from February to April. Good Windsor flavour and fine freezer.

French Beans
The Prince: Long pods, tender picked young and keeps going longest if continuously picked. Fewer plants supply all your beans.

Sprite: Completely stringless. Continental flavour and a good freezer.

Purley King: The best drying haricot bean, related to the Heinz 'Baked Bean' variety. Also a good french bean to cook whole.

Runner Beans
Enorma: A big bean, 21-inch (53cm) pods, fine flavour and a good freezer.

White Achievement: Rather smaller pods, but excellent dried as a butter bean or frozen.

The Czar: The best flavoured white runner bean to dry as a butter bean pre-1914.

Blue Lake: A climbing French bean, with stringless pods and white seeds. Grows more dried 'haricot beans' than the bush types.

Beet
Boltardy: Slow to bolt from early sowings.

Detroit Little Ball: A fast round beet for summer sowings and stores very well.

Dobbies Purple: Formerly Dell's purple, a dark red beetroot grown for flavour ever since 1885.

Broccoli

Autumn Spear: The sprouting broccoli to eat from September to November. Like all this group, has some clubroot resistance. Purple Sprouting: To eat from March to May, there are early and late forms; experiment to find the best succession in your district.

Brussels sprouts

Bedford Winter Harvest: The longest-cropping variety, in production from October to February. Survives hard winters.

Cabbage

April: One of the best spring cabbages.

Summer Monarch: A fast summer cabbage excellent shredded in salads.

Red Drumhead: The only red cabbage the EEC regulations allow, adds colour and flavour to winter salads. Too good to pickle. Cook it and enjoy it.

Winningstadt: A fine old autumn cabbage to eat from August to November.

January King: For December to March.

Ormskirk Rearguard: Savoy, crinkly-leaf type, to eat from Christmas right on into spring. Stands hard winters.

Carrots

Early Nantes: A fast, stump-rooted kind for spring and summer sowings.

Chantenay Red Cored Favourite: Heavy yielding maincrop that stores well.

Cauliflowers

All the Year Round: A large, white, curded variety which can be sown to be ready at any time of year in the South.

Walcheren Winter (formerly a broccoli): Comes through hard winters and is ready in April.

Celeriac

Tellus: A much improved variety of the old species.

Celery

Golden Self-Blanching: To eat from August till frost.

Solid White: Needs blanching, ready from October to January.

Cucumbers

Burpless Tasty Green: A cucumber to grow outdoors, not of greenhouse quality. Resists mildew.

Kale

Tall Green Curled: The last survivor of the Scots kales. Very hardy. Supplies Vitamins C and A to go with haggis and porridge.

Thousand Head: The hardiest plain-leaved variety. Young shoots to eat in spring, and the most productive winter poultry greenfood.

Kohl rabi

White Vienna: Sow for succession and eat small, raw or cooked.

Leeks

Musselburgh: A good, all-round, very hardy leek that lasts till April.

Lettuce

Fortune: A quick-growing cabbage kind to sow for succession up to July.

Avondefiance: For July/August sowing, resists mildew and root aphids.

Avoncrisp: For earlier sowing. Also mildew and aphid resisting.

Windermere: The finest 'frilly' lettuce, quick to mature and slowest to bolt, lasting a month from a single sowing. Large and stout midribs – a good one weighs 1 lb (450g),(no good commercially, for lettuces are not sold by weight, but excellent for gardeners).

Little Gem: A quick-growing, compact cos lettuce with a fine flavour. Sow March to mid-July.

Winter Density: Sow in August as the hardiest winter-cos variety.

Imperial Winter: Sow in September to heart in the spring. The hardiest winter cabbage kind.

Onions

Bedfordshire Champion: A long-keeping, heavy-cropping, mild variety. Buy Red Italian for a real, strong onion taste. Still legal in Italy, so buy it on holiday in Europe.

Express Yellow: The best of the Japanese varieties to sow in August and eat as early as July, ripening off faster than sets, to dry and keep.

Solidity: A large, flat onion resistant to bolting; sow outdoors in September and transplant in spring, for a fast finish, ripening in time for green manure cropping afterwards.

Sturon: A round, long-keeping variety also available as sets (small bulbs) for early spring planting.

White Lisbon: The traditional spring onion to sow from

March to September. Plants from early sowings, can be transplanted to grow onions for cooking quickly, if those stored have failed to keep.

Parsley
Paramount-Imperial Curled: A closely curled kind and the hardiest, needing no protection in hard northern winters.

Parsnip
White Gem: Good flavour and shorter roots than Tender and True and the show varieties, so easier to lift for storing. Resistant to canker.

Peas
Early Onward: A heavy cropper to sow in succession from March to June. Two-feet (60cm) high so needs only low support. Freezes well.

Kelvedon Wonder: Early but excellent for June-July sowings because it resists the mildew common in late cropping peas. Eighteen inches (45cm).

Meteor: The hardiest early pea for November sowing to produce a really early picking with or without cloches. Eighteen inches (45cm).

Pilot: The best drying pea, sown in February or March. Tall (3½ft or a metre high), with a heavy crop to leave on and dry, as well as eating early as a normal pea.

Radishes
Cherry Belle: The radish that lasts longest from a single sowing without growing hot and woody.

Black Spanish Round or Long: White radish flavoured flesh, black skin, for cooking or raw eating in winter.

China Rose: Looks like a giant French Breakfast radish, red and white. Both excellent grated in winter salads.

Salsify
Giant: Can be lifted and stored or stay in the ground. Young shoots in the spring like asparagus.

Scorzonera
Russian Giant: Black skinned. A different flavour and rather easier to peel. Just as hardy as salsify.

Swedes
Western Perfection: Fast growing to cricket-ball size to dig as required.

Sweetcorn
First of All: The fastest finisher for the British climate; produces a freezerful, even in the north.

Tomatoes
    Harbinger: Won the John Innes Trial for the outdoor variety
    with the most ripe before 6 September in 1942. First-class
    flavour, thin skin and the best of all to ripen off the plant.
Turnips
    Snowball: A fast, white variety to reach eating size in about
    six weeks. Leave them in longer at wider spacing to delight
    your pony.
    Golden Ball: A yellow-fleshed kind also for quick growing,
    and a contrasting colour grated on the salad. Good keeper.

Species, like Miner's lettuce (*Claytonia perfoliata)* and herbs,
are not in peril in the EEC so are not on this list of varieties
worth saving on their merits. A revival of interest, especially in
the older varieties, could well keep them in the catalogues
indefinitely.

Think ahead to summer
January is the time to think ahead to the summer, and do every
job that can be done to give more time in the headlong rush of
March and April. Start saving the smaller sizes of tins, or
collect from neighbours if you do not use any, taking the bottoms
out with a rotary tin opener, soaking the paper off and giving
them a coat inside and out of black bitumen paint, ready to
place over your carrots after thinning. The carrot-fly *(Psila
rosea)* comes in low like a cruise missile to lay its eggs close to
where the leaves start from the ground and the tin can baffle it.
This is one of the many counter-measures used by organic
gardeners against this pest, but it is, like all the others, not 100
per cent successful, and the inorganic answers are not much
better. The tin trick is very successful against surface caterpillars
or cutworms, which are the larvae of the heart and dart moth,
the turnip moth, the diamond black moth and the yellow
underwing, which will clear a bed of newly planted cabbages in
a night.
    If you find seedlings vanishing overnight from the attacks of
these nocturnal caterpillars, and you have the tins already
painted, you can slip them on and beat the pests. The reason for
painting is firstly to stop the tins rusting and keep them smooth
to provide no grip for climbing caterpillars and secondly
because the black surface absorbs the heat and warms the
young carrots ahead, as well as keeping the wind off them.

Compost cabbages and their pests

An even more useful pest-control measure against the mealy cabbage aphis *(Brevicoryne brassicae)* and the cabbage white fly *(Aleyrodes proletella)* can begin now. Stretch the garden line where you will be sowing the first runner beans in May and take out a trench eight inches (20cm) wide and deep for the first row. As your cabbages, Brussels sprouts and broccoli finish, *dig* – do not pull – the stumps up and spread them along the bottom of the trench to make a loose layer about four inches (10cm) thick. Empty your daily kitchen waste on top of them, which is far better than adding them to the dormant compost heap in winter where they can attract rats. Cover each bucketful with soil at once, so the birds do not steal the waste or strew it round the garden, and tread it down, filling up the trench completely before digging the one for the next row beside it. If you dig several trenches at once the sides crumble as you stumble about with the full bucket. If any stumps show clubroot, chop the root off and dump it in the dustbin, for stems do not carry spores.

As the kitchen waste decays between the stumps, the soil will sink and need topping up before the beans are sown or planted; then as the stumps themselves rot the soil will sink further, leaving a shallow trough to fill with the hose when the beans are tall and thirsty, for the shock of cold mains water on the foliage may mean dropped blossoms. When the crop is cleared, the stumps will have decayed to lasting black humus, for you have made long, narrow compost heaps, activated by the surplus nitrogen fixed by the bacteria in the bean roots. Bash the last of the broccoli stems with an axe back on a concrete path so that they decay faster to help the last sown beans.

The extra value of this trick lies in killing the over-wintering eggs of the two increasingly awkward cabbage-tribe pests that are helped by those who leave their Brussels-sprout stems in to grow 'spring greens' on top. The nine-star, perennial broccoli is also responsible for some of the increase because, like the perennial kale, it provides winter quarters for millions of these pests. Kitchen waste alone can be used for pea trenches, especially for Pilot, the drying pea, for their bacteria do not seem vigorous enough to deal with Brussels-sprout stems. Those who do not have a 'poultry bucket' for potato peelings would do well to exclude these because they can grow from only the eyes in the peel and potatoes among the peas are weeds that should be taken out before they swamp the row.

Feed birds with your pests

If January is dry and mild enough to allow digging, turn over the ground where you had carrots, onions or cabbages, unless this is under green manure, to give the robins a chance to peck up the chrysalids of the cabbage, carrot and onion flies, and between the raspberry canes to give them another go at the pupae of the raspberry beetle *(Byturus tormentosus)*. Robins' eyes can pick out pest pupae which we cannot tell from tiny stones, and this is why they follow us round the garden whenever we are digging. Almost every garden is the territory of a pair of robins, and it is possible to feed these useful birds rather than the starlings, by getting your local birds used to taking food from your hand. Wild bird food for insectivorous species can be bought, or grated cheese supplied in really cold weather to keep your friendly neighbourhood pest eaters surviving.

The tit family – blue, great and coal – are even more easily fed and enlisted as winter helpers. Obtain a piece of fat about four inches (10cm) square from your butcher, who will hopefully give it free, and hang it from the tip of a six-foot (2m) bamboo cane thrust slantways into the rose bed. It should hang about a foot (30cm) above the bushes. There will be room for at most two tits on the fat, and when food is scarce there may be as many as ten others waiting for their turns to perch and peck. These will fill in time by searching the gnarled bark round the bases of the bushes for the eggs of greenfly, so there will be none to hatch next summer and no need to spray.

This is perhaps the ideal organic gardening trick, because it costs nothing, is less work than spraying even with a safe pesticide, and does no harm whatever to the environment. It is also a good idea to hang small pieces of fat (small because large have room for hungry starlings, or too many tits so they neglect their aphid eating) below ornamental cherries. These harbour the cherry blackfly *(Myzus cerasi)* which is resistant to ladybirds, and Viburnums of any species, also Euonymus, for these are the winter home of the blackfly of broad beans *(Aphis fabae)*. It is also worth hanging fat well below your apple trees (where the starlings are unable to get it), so that the local tits will clean up anything that they can reach in the way of pest eggs.

Fruit care in January

The first fruit problem of the year is to remember *not* to use the new secateurs you have been given for Christmas to prune stone fruit. Apricots, cherries, damsons, greengages, nectarines, peaches and plums are all not for pruning, because the spores of several fungi causing the condition known as 'dieback' are blowing about. Wait till May when this risk will be over. Even apples and pears, traditionally winter-pruned, are better done in February or early March, to dodge *Sclerotina*, the fungus responsible for brown storage rot, which keeps commercial growers spraying from July till picking time. It is no more work to prune a little later and costs nothing.

Look carefully round the orchard in January to see if there are any fruits still hanging on, withered and lonely. They can hold the spores of a number of fungi that are better taken off with a long-arm pruner, or picked from steps, and brought in to burn on a cheerful fire than leaving them releasing millions of microscopic troublemakers next spring. If a cherry still has any leaves hanging on in January, pick them and burn them too, because this shows cherry-leaf scorch fungus *(Gnomonia erythrostoma)* with spores waiting to infect the opening leaf buds. On small trees, picking off is possible, but larger ones need spraying.

The best all-round fungicide for organic gardeners is Burgundy Mixture, for its copper does no harm to anything other than fungi (unlike lime-sulphur which harms many varieties known as 'sulphur-shy' and kills useful predators such as *Anthocoris nemorum* and its relatives) and it reaches the ground in trace-element quantities. It can be bought ready made-up, but if copper sulphate can be obtained, dissolve half a pound in a gallon (250g in 5 litres) of boiling water and one pound of washing soda in a gallon (500g in 5 litres) of cold. Mix the two with a further three gallons (15 litres) of cold water in a plastic container, because the copper can react with metal. Spray this mixture on in December and January, when the beds are at their most dormant, and nothing but fungi will be harmed. In addition to cherry-leaf scorch, it is the best answer to peach-leaf curl *(Taphrina deformans)* and the less common cherry-leaf curl *(T. minor)*, and is also quite effective against apple scab *(Venturia inaequalis)*. A cheaper and easier remedy for this one is urine sprayed neat on the branches, for the 2.3 per cent of urea it contains is just as effective from every gardener's private supply as the synthetic chemical sold in bulk to commercial fruit growers.

January is the month to destroy the plum-curl aphis *(Brachy-caudus helichrysi)*, which is extremely difficult to kill at its summer stage inside the curled leaves, but easy if you catch it when it has just hatched in January and February and is creeping into the bud scales, and before it starts to multiply like microchips. Soft soap is hard to buy today, but the paraffin emulsion used in the past can be made with soap flakes. Dissolve 4 oz (110g) of these in a pint (0.5 litre) of hot water, and add to this 16 fluid oz (0.75 litre) of ordinary paraffin. Stir this up rapidly with enough extra water (cold) to make a gallon (4.5 litres) and spray it on. This is also effective against the hibernating stage of American blight or woolly aphid *(Eriosoma lanigerum)* which is *not* repelled by nasturtiums trained up the trees – by the time these flower the creature has gone into hiding. Spraying with paraffin emulsion at the right time will hit it hard.

One of the last January jobs among the fruit is to take off the suckers which spring up round so many trees, especially if they are grafted on the old Mussel stock for stone fruit and ornamental trees of the same family, which can come up all over the lawn. Dig away the soil round the tree until you can grip the sucker shoot firmly and *twist* it off as though you were unscrewing it. This tears out the 'heel' from which it springs and once this is destroyed there will be no more trouble. Where suckers have been cut again and again with secateurs and made a large mass, it is worth taking a large adjustable spanner as though you were a mechanic rather than a gardener, and 'unscrewing' the sucker base to burn, because these are favourite hiding places for many pests.

5.

February

The celery will be finished, but otherwise the available foods are the same as in January though the pumpkins may well give out before the end of the month. It is rarely that pumpkins can be kept after Christmas, because they miss the long, hot autumns of the USA and other warmer places which toughen and seal their skins. Inspect them as they hang, in the nylon net bags greengrocers have free for the asking, from the rafters in the attic with the onions. They may well have soft spots which show decay and should be sawn open and the firm orange flesh salvaged for soups and eating as a far better vegetable than a marrow. Never hang pumpkins up by their stalks – these tear away, leaving a wood that starts decay.

Pumpkins cannot compare with potatoes for concentrated food value (see Table 12), but the Japanese varieties are worth finding. As the seed keeps ten years it is worth buying plenty, for only a few are sown each season. Save the largest and fattest seeds from the most mature stored specimens in the attic.

Start sprouting seed potatoes
The seed potatoes should have arrived by now and begin their twelve-week stay in the 'chitting trays'. These should be the non-returnable wood trays with raised corners that hold imported grapes and tomatoes and are worth paying for because they last several seasons. Set the seed tubers 'rose end' (the end with the eyes in) upwards, and stack the trays – one on top of the

Available for eating	Family	Sowing	Planting
Artichokes, Jerusalem	3	–	February-March
Beans (dried or frozen)	7	May-June	–
Beet (leaf)	2	April	–
Beet (stored)	2	May	–
Broccoli (heading)	4	May	July
Brussels sprouts	4	May	June-July
Cabbage	4	June	July
Carrots (stored)	12	May	–
Celeriac	12	March	May
Hamburg parsley	12	March-April	–
Kale	4	April	June-July
Lamb's-lettuce	13	July-August	–
Landcress	4	August-September	–
Leeks	8	April	July
Lettuce	3	March-July	–
Miner's lettuce	10	July-August	–
Onions (stored)	8	March	–
Parsnips	12	February-March	–
Peas (dried or frozen)	7	January-May	–
Potatoes (stored)	11	–	April-May
Pumpkins	5	April	May
Radish, Chinese	4	July	–
Salsify	3	March-April	–
Scorzonera	3	March-April	–
Spinach (winter)	2	September	–
Swedes (stored)	4	July	–
Sweetcorn (frozen)	6	April-May	–
Tomatoes (bottled)	11	–	May-June
Turnips (stored)	4	June-July	–

other if you have to save space – in a frost-free shed, under a greenhouse staging or in a spare bedroom, for they need light and a temperature of 8-10°C.

The ideal seed potato is the size of the smallest grade of hen's egg, but today the growers expect to sell their whole crop at seed price, instead of taking the eating potato rate for the large ones. Tubers bigger than 'large'-egg size are best cut. Slice them from the rose end down, leaving three good eyes on each half, and dip the cut surface in garden lime to dry it and prevent decay. Set the cut tubers in the trays, with the cut surfaces away from each other, and inspect them at intervals to remove any that have

Table 12: Comparative food values of potato, pumpkin and marrow

	Potato (boiled) %	Japanese pumpkin %	American pumpkin %	Marrow %
Moisture	76.40	86.90	97.2	97.8
Carbohydrate	19.70	8.10	1.40	1.40
Protein	2.10	1.80	0.50	0.40
Calcium	1–1	0.04	0.03	1–1
Phosphorus	1–1	0.04	0.01	1–1
Carotene m. g. per kilogram	1–1	27.00	5.90	1–1

decayed. So long as the sprouts are sturdy, potatoes lose nothing by waiting in the chitting trays for even sixteen weeks, in savage springs, or waiting for a winter crop to finish.

Though the variety of potatoes sold by greengrocers must now be written on the bag, the wholesaler will have treated them with an anti-sprouting chemical, so they cannot be a source of cheap seed. Organically grown potatoes will not have any chemically treatment, and can be safely bought and put straight in the chitting trays in February.

Today there is less and less choice of potatoes, now that the most famous British seedsman stocks only two varieties. There is one potato specialist left, Donald MacLean, Dornoch Farm, Crieff, Perthshire, who stocks about 350 kinds and he sells by post to those who wish to try a variety and then save their own seed if they like it. There is a constant procession of new varieties from the plant-breeding centres, with greater yields, resistance to diseases and qualities like high dry matter. Flavour, however, is a question of taste. The following varieties are all available today and at least some will be stocked by garden centres for the next few years.

Potato varieties

First earlies
Arran Pilot: Heavy early cropper, some scab resistance.

Duke of York: Not so fast. Fine flavour, yellow flesh and will keep till April left in to grow large. Dig the first for scraping new, and eat the last baked in their jackets.

Epicure: Heavy early cropper. Deep eyes. Fine flavour, recovers best from destruction of shoots by late frosts, so good in the north.

Home Guard: High yield. High dry matter, some scab resistance. Picks up any taint from soil, especially BHC. Safe grown organically.

Sharpes Express: High dry matter, very fine flavour, lower yield early. Will keep left in to grow large.

Ulster Sceptre: High yield early. Best drought resister.

Second earlies

Maris Peer: Resists scab, high dry matter. Some blight resistance.

Wilja: High yielder. Some blight resistance.

Maincrops

Arran Consul: The potato that grows old gracefully. Late sprouting. Good cooker.

Desiree: Pink skinned. Good flavour and cooking quality, the most popular maincrop today, beating King Edward. Resists drought but the most subject to scab. Good keeper.

Kerr's Pink: Has the thickest foliage for weed suppression, and is a chip-shop favourite, because the chips do not discolour without water.

Maris Piper: Fine flavour. Resists *Globodera rostochiensis*, one potato eelworm, but not *G. pallida*, the other one. A good maincrop.

Record: The finest flavour maincrop. High dry matter.

Stormont Enterprise: Drought and slug resistant.

Plant artichokes now

Globe artichokes are like asparagus – not worth the trouble in small gardens for the food produced from their space, but the Jerusalem artichoke, with its knobby, cream-coloured tubers, is easy, hardy and very welcome to anyone allergic to potatoes. The best variety is Fuseau, which is the least knobby, and a tapered shape, which is scarce. Artichokes have no disease or viruses and greengrocers are the best source of supply. Once you find Fuseau or a less-knobby strain of the common type, you can keep it going indefinitely.

Start the bed by digging in a barrow-load of manure or compost to four square yards (or metres), and plant your tubers in six-inch (15 cm) deep trowel holes, eighteen inches (45 cm) apart and three feet (1 metre) between rows. Keep down the weeds by hoeing and as they grow tall like sunflowers, they will need stakes at the ends and middle of the rows so that strings can be run each side of them in windy gardens. Once the plants are over a foot high they need no more hoeing and can be lifted as required from November onwards, leaving enough to replant the bed next February or March.

The only pest of artichokes is a small, grey, root aphis which will be found hiding on the tubers at lifting time. The answer is to move the bed and wash the tubers in the cheapest powerful insecticide before replanting. Simmer ¾ lb (350 g) of filter-tip cigarette ends in a gallon (4.5 litres) of water for half an hour – these are about 0.1 per cent nicotine and a serious risk to the health of pests, from aphids to caterpillars. Strain the clear, brown liquid through nylon tights, and use it neat for caterpillars or diluted with a further gallon of water for aphids. Non-smokers can obtain cigarette ends from pubs, cinemas and bingo halls, storing their stock in a large tin, for nicotine is a deadly poison, but no one will mistake your hoarded ends for sweets. Boil it up as required, keep it off your skin and treat it with caution. Nicotine is used by organic gardeners because it spares ladybirds and their larvae, and breaks down in forty-eight hours. The cigarette-end concoction costs nothing, so can be used freely when required.

The dried stems of artichokes can be cut for light staking, or even compost in November, but you cannot cut down the growing stems for compost without harming the crop of tubers which should be about the same as early potatoes from the same area, far better from tubers lifted and replanted each year than left to crowd in a neglected bed. The analysis is very like that of a potato but they hold about seven times as much calcium. This is excellent for those on a milk-free diet, because there is no oxalic acid to lock it up.

Try and get your family accustomed to eating new vegetables – artichokes are so easy and nutritious that it is worth learning to like their rather smokey taste. It is unfortunate children whose parents proclaim, 'Of course all they *really* like is frozen peas, chips, fish fingers and ice-cream', because they will grow up to be just customers, rather than experimenting gardeners who enjoy a wide range of foods.

Remember rhubarb

February is also rhubarb-planting time, and after fifteen years or more the familiar nameless shapes at the bottom of the garden show rotten hollows in the black surface stems which are signs of wear. Select the strongest with fat pink buds at the ends and cut them off with about nine inches (23 cm) of thick stem without rotten hollows. There is no need to rotate rhubarb, but if you can spare another space for a permanent planting, you can remove your offsets or crowns for the new bed, and leave the old in production until its successor can take over. Newly planted crowns must have a year without picking to get established.

Scatter 2 lb (1 kg) of bonemeal to the square yard (metre) on the new bed, then dig it over with care to remove perennial weed roots, tucking a barrow-load of compost or well-rotted manure to two square yards well down in the trench bottoms. Then plant your crown upright with the bud just peeping through the surface, two feet (60 cm) apart and three (a metre) between rows. There is room to grow two staggered rows of lettuces between each two of rhubarb the first summer.

The best variety is Glaskin's Perpetual, which is the lowest in oxalic acid so it can be eaten even in August, but never strip a crown, because even rhubarb needs its rest and the leaves are gathering energy to feed the roots for next spring's forcing, for it is the easiest and most welcome first fruit in every garden. Early Victoria and Timperley Early are both excellent flavour kinds.

Existing beds should have been covered thickly with leaf-mould in November, and they are now ready to force. Once this was done under bottomless buckets or brown tin-baths, but even rhubarb must enter the plastic age, for the large earthenware drainpipes that also served are now scarce and costly. Find plastic containers, not necessarily buckets, such as the drums in which many industrial products are delivered. They should be large enough to fit over a thriving crown, about 12-15 inches (30-45 cm) across the open top, and about the same height or taller. Melt a hole in the bottom about two inches in diameter over a candle flame to provide light for the shoots to draw towards, and coat the outside of the tin with black bitumen paint. Plastic is not sufficiently opaque to drive the shoots towards the light, and the dark surface will concentrate the spring sunlight, to give you solar-heated rhubarb rather more quickly than from the bottomless buckets of the past.

Sowings for February

The 500-gauge polythene sheet used to cover manure heaps is also of value in gaining growing time in spring. Dig over the beds where onions, carrots, lettuces, parsnips and early peas will be sown in March, and cover these with the useful polythene weighed down with bricks or long, heavy wood, to warm up and escape the rain. It is always a question of whether it is better to wait till the soil has warmed and the tide of spring is flowing, or to go ahead and get the work done before the rush, risking cold drying winds and savage mice and birds.

Parsnips can be sown towards the end of February, and this early sowing is worth it for those who need to eat small roots as early as August. The main crop for storing should wait till the second week in April because later sowings lower the canker risk and store better. Start the bed with 1 lb (500g) of lime and 8 oz (250g) fish or meat and bonemeal to four square yards (metres) unless the soil had compost the previous year, fork it lightly in and rake level before sowing the seed in clusters of four at nine-inch (23cm) intervals along inch-deep (2.5cm) furrows a foot (30cm) apart. Because the parsnips will take about twenty days to show and this is time for them to be swamped by weeds, sow radishes in the gaps between the clusters before closing the furrows with the hoe blade.

The radishes will be up fast to pull as the first new salad crop of the season, and when it is clear which is the best in each bunch of parsnips, the others can be pulled out to give it room. Beyond hoeing to keep the weeds down the parsnips need little further attention. They may be attacked by celery-leaf miner, which tunnels the leaves in pale-green, wandering streaks. Spray with nicotine, which gets through the thin skin of the leaf, or, if only a few leaves suffer, pick them off. Do not grow lovage in your herb bed because this perennial vegetable harbours the celery-leaf miner through the winter and can start an attack earlier than the usual August.

Another crop that gains from an early start is onions from sets. Prepare the ground as for the parsnips – in fact they can well go next to them on the root bed – but go over their ground, treading it firm, raking level and then rolling it, because onions must have firm soil to push against when they heave themselves out to sit on the surface and ripen in the sun. Even on a heavy clay, if the soil has been dried out under plastic, it will not puddle provided it has had lime and humus. Plant the near pea-sized bulblets six inches (15cm) apart and a foot (30cm) between rows, using a dibber, twisting off the dry tops so that nothing shows when the soil is firmed back with the dibber point. If the dry top shows the sparrows will assume it is good nesting material and uproot all the sets.

The first peas can go in during February, Early Onward to follow the first autumn-sown Meteor, and are best tipped into a basin and swirled with paraffin as a bird and mouse discourager. If there are no trenches ready with winter kitchen waste, take out a six-inch (15cm) deep trench and tread the partly rotted top of a compost heap into the bottom three inches (8cm) then fill up with soil. Sow the peas two inches (5cm) apart in two rows with three inches (8cm) between them, covered with about an inch of soil.

Wire pea-guards should be bent over the rows and blocked at the ends. This not only keeps the birds off, but makes it safe to set mousetraps in the row so you can catch field mice without harming your robins. Peas appreciate the hollow made as the compost or refuse sinks to hold water, for in dry years each sowing lasts longer if it is given generous hosings.

The pea rows can be thirty inches (75cm) apart, which leaves room to make the first and most useful sowing of a summer spinach such as Nobel or Jovita, down the middle of the space between the rows in a half-inch deep (13mm) furrow. Thin to six inches (15cm) apart and eat the thinnings, then pick the leaves hard for salads, for at this time of year they are low in oxalic acid, as rhubarb is, and up to 79mg calcium per 100 grams, which is three times more than they contain cooked.

Countering clubroot
Summer cabbage and summer cauliflower are both worth sowing in February, under pea guards because of the bird risk to the young plants; sow them in the cabbage-tribe section of the rotation and aim to keep these two to the minimum. Clubroot is most active in summer, and if lettuces can provide your summer green vegetables rather than cabbages, the lower your clubroot level will be.

The latest recommendation from the National Vegetable Research Station against clubroot is to give a really heavy dressing of lime, 2 lb per square yard (1 kg a square metre) to the cabbage section of the rotation, dig it in, and then sow your plants. If this is done repeatedly there is a risk that too much lime will lock up the boron in the soil. This causes crown canker in beet, with the centre leaves dying and the roots rotting from the outside; brown patches on cauliflower curds; brown hearts in turnips and tomato fruit, with uneven ripening and brown corky spots. The answer is to dissolve an ounce (25 g) of borax (which is a mixture of salts of boron and sodium, used for gargling and which makes an excellent ant poison mixed thoroughly with equal parts of icing sugar and left under cover where ants will find it) in two gallons (9 litres) of hot water and water it on over ten square yards (or metres). These problems, especially fruit spot in tomatoes, have happened in very chalky gardens, but a little borax would be a minor problem compared with the value of conquering clubroot.

Fruit in February
The winter pruning of apples consists of shortening the leaders, which are the longest and strongest shoots that grew last summer on every branch, by a third of their length. Then snip off their lesser contemporaries after the third, fourth or fifth bud – whichever points away from the centre of the tree. If the tree is a tip bearer, carrying its fruit on the ends of the branches like Worcester Pearmain, Blenheim Orange or Irish Peach, all it will need is to have the weakest branch or two sawn out each year together with any that are crossing, crowding or have dead wood on them.

Normal trees, like Cox's Orange Pippin and James Grieve also need any branches that are crossing or crowding the centre sawn out now, but this and ordinary pruning are less important than a thorough search for canker, which is caused by the fungus *Nectria galligena* infecting damaged bark from the scrape of a small boy's climbing boot, a graze from a careless pruning saw, or wounds from airgun pellets fired at bullfinches, or damage from the tiny punctures in the bark made by woolly aphid.

The cankers grow like craters in the bark surrounded by rough ridges and gradually girdle a branch until this dies. When small branches and spurs are cankered, cut these right out until the wood shows white, but with large branches – especially at forks – cut away the canker, using a chisel to get into clean wood, and coat the cut with Arbortect to keep out further spores. Take the branch right out if the tree can spare it.

Apple scab can also be seen on the bark of year-old shoots, that is, the sections of the spurs and leaders left at last year's pruning time. The smooth young bark will be wrinkled, torn and split, and the exposed portions will be covered with black patches that produce the spores. Prune these out, taking out the small, spurred branches with a pruning saw, and, like all apple prunings, burn them and hoard the ashes as these will be high in potash.

Then spray with Burgundy Mixture at its dormant stage against both scab and apple mildew *(Podosphaera leucotricha)*. The last is best sought at blossom time, and looks like a white powder on the unfolding buds in spring. Remove any infected spurs and burn, for they will not fruit anyway. There are many mildew spores in the ordinary wood buds, and pruning removes these; if tip bearers show mildew, shorten their shoots by about three inches (80cm). Another disease to watch for when the blossom opens is blossom wilt *(Sclerotinia laxa)*, when young leaves round the trusses wilt and die, followed by the blossom itself. The only answer is to prune out the attacked spurs and burn them. Infected spurs may have small grey cushions of fungus on them, so should be cut out completely. Luckily this disease is rare.

Pears are pruned in the same way as apples, and should be sprayed in February, before their earlier blossom starts, with Burgundy Mixture against pear scab, pear-leaf blister *(Taphrina bullata)*, which is related to peach-leaf curl, and *Phytophthora cactorum*, which produces brown patches on the fruit. It is even more important to remove mummified fruit left on from last year because this harbours pear midge as well as *Phytophthora* spores.

The pear-leaf blister mite *(Eriophyes piyi)* breeds five generations a year and in February, when it is waking up and still hibernating under the bud scales, paraffin emulsion will catch it when the leaves are just beginning to open. It is better to wait till you see green or reddish blisters on the leaves. Pick them off and burn them so you stop the first generation, for the fifth can strip the leaves off a tree.

The American gooseberry mildew *(Spaerotheca mors-*

uvae) is the curse of many gardens, and though the spores are tough, they are spreading in February. A remedy that has been found effective in Canada is to spray the bushes with neat urine just before the leaf buds open, and three weeks later with urine diluted with three parts of water. In Canada the neat urine spray for apple and pear scab is given just before the leaf buds open.

6.

March

Once it was said that March came in like a lion and went out like a lamb, and that a peck of March dust was worth half a load of hay compared with a full load for a swarm of bees in May. Today our springs are dry and cold, but it is still worth neglecting the lawn and the television to get as much sown as possible, even if there are losses and we must sow again in April. Sowing for the long-term, slow-growing, cabbage-tribe plants like sprouting broccoli and savoys can wait till April, so can beet because these store better small. Those whose stores are running low and who need new supplies urgently will get in a small batch in March and more later.

Vegetable sowing and growing in March
Broad beans are potash hungry and can take as much as 8 oz (220g) a square yard (or metre) of wood ashes. This will be available more rapidly than rock potash, which should have gone on in the autumn before crops like beans, potatoes and tomatoes are planted. The Sutton, sown a foot (30cm) apart each way at monthly intervals, will take over from the autumn-sown Aquadulce Claudia, with the last sowing in July. Plant with a dibber two inches (5cm) deep and hoe perhaps once before their bushiness takes over. Eat the first in the pods and shell them as they get tougher, clearing each batch for compost. Only experience teaches exactly how many of everything a family needs, even if they need broad beans right through the summer.

Available for eating	Family	Sowing	Planting
Artichokes, Jerusalem	3	–	February-March
Beans (dried or frozen)	7	May-June	–
Beet (stored)	2	May	–
Broccoli (early sprouting)	4	April	June
Brussels sprouts	4	May	June-July
Cabbage	4	June	July
Carrots (stored)	12	May	–
Celeriac	12	March	May
Kale	4	April	June-July
Lamb's-lettuce	13	July-August	–
Landcress	4	August-September	–
Leeks	8	April	July
Lettuce	3	March-July	–
Miner's lettuce	10	July-August	–
Onions (stored)	8	March	–
Peas (dried or frozen)	7	January-May	–
Potatoes (stored)	11	–	April-May
Radish, Chinese	4	July	–
Rhubarb	9	April	February
Salsify	3	March-April	–
Scorzonera	3	March-April	–
Spinach (winter)	2	September	–
Swedes (stored)	4	July	–
Sweetcorn (frozen)	6	April-May	–
Tomatoes (bottled)	11	–	May-June
Turnips (stored)	4	June-July	–

The Windsor and Longpod beans need more room, but produce a heavier crop. Sow them three inches (8cm) deep eight inches (20cm) apart along the line, then move this six inches (15cm) down the garden and plant another row, spaced to come in between the others. The staggered rows hold each other up, though stakes and string at the end of rows are advisable later; if you need more than a double row, allow thirty inches (75cm) between them for picking room.

Broad beans are easy, but the more beans the fewer peas, and both Pilot for drying, and Early Onward or Kelvedon Wonder for freezing, should be sown in March, just like the earlies in February. Remember that the drying peas are going to stay longer in their room than those picked green, and that peas eaten fresh (ideally raw in salads) are nicer than frozen. The spacing is standard, because as the peas and beans clear, they are just cut off at ground level to leave their nitrogen-rich roots in the soil ready for the cabbage-tribe crops to plant directly without digging in the firm soil.

Freezers, like fire, are good servants but bad masters and filling a freezer with frozen peas will give a poor diet compared with the crops you could have grown for fresh eating or shed storage in the same space. There is the cost of the current and the investment in the freezer. People with allergies, who must have a rotation of different meats, as well as meat eaters, will get the best value from fetching meat ready cut up in meal-sized packs from an organic farm. Freezers are useful time savers, for baking wholemeal bread ahead and cooking for a big weekend, but if we fill them with root vegetables which would just as well keep in ashes, sand or peat, or tomatoes and bush fruit which could be bottled, we are wasting an asset. Bought ·frozen vegetables may have been treated with substances that give a brighter colour but lock up useful minerals so they pass wasted from our bodies, apart from the question of allergic reactions. Our own frozen foods may well be many shades less colourful than bought, but we know exactly what is in them.

If we sow a fast round beet like Detroit Little Ball in March we can eat it in June, and June sowings will be cricket-ball size for storing by October. The policy for those who want to eat beetroot over the longest period is to sow single rows and start eating them at golf-ball size, sowing extra rows later for storing. Sow the large seeds like tiny, dried raspberries in pairs at six-inch (15 cm) intervals along furrows eight inches (20 cm) apart, which leaves just enough room for hoeing. As beet belong to 'No. 2' they can be grown without rotation with spinach and the other vegetables marked with asterisks in Table 1, anywhere they will fit in.

Carrots, too, can be sown in two batches – one now to take over from the shrinking hoard in store and a summer sowing for storage, which may be smaller than normal, but will dodge the worst of the carrot-fly. They need a fine, sandy soil or a clay that has been given ample leaf-mould or compost and are best following a crop that was manured the previous year. Dry the soil out under polythene, mix the fine seed with eight times its bulk of fine bonemeal so that as little as ½ oz (14g) of seed fills 200 feet (60m) of ½-inch (1cm) deep furrows eight inches (20cm) apart, and the cream colour of the bonemeal shows up well against the dark soil. Pelleted seed is sold so the tiny seeds can be sown singly with less carrot-fly risk, for it is the scent of the thinnings that attracts these, but the coat of clay and chemicals that enlarges it also keeps out the moisture in dry springs, which can lose the crop anyway. Early carrots should be short, fat and fast, so Early Nantes or Amsterdam Forcing are the best for these first sowings.

Salsify and scorzonera have long, large seeds and it is easy to sow them individually at eight-inch (20cm) intervals along inch-deep (2.5cm) furrows eight inches (20cm) apart. They can be lifted and stored or eaten as required, but sow extra salsify because of the value of the young shoots you could be eating now. Surround the salsify bed reserved for forcing with foot-high (30cm) wire-netting (brick reinforcement netting can be bought from a builders' merchant, which costs less and lasts longer) stapled to short posts. Fill up the enclosure with leaf-mould when the salsify leaves have died down, and scrape it away in March when the young leaves – like wide, folded grass blades – show through the leaf-mould. Pick them and either chop and serve raw in salads or cook as a spinach with an asparagus flavour. The roots taste of oysters, hence the popular name of 'oyster plant', but they could equally well be called 'no-trouble asparagus' because of the value of the spring shoots. These continue in production until June, when they run up and flower with sweet sultan-like blooms about two inches (5cm) across. Like scorzonera, which has yellow, daisy flowers and wide, hairy, non-edible leaves, salsify is a species and if a few flowers are allowed to ripen their dandelion-like seedheads, enough will grow to sow and give away for years. They do not cross-pollinate because, like elephants and rhinoceroses, they have different chromosomes.

Salsify foliage is too good to compost if you have chickens, because the flower stems are the green food they like best of all, perhaps because it is so rich in iron, without oxalic acid to lock it up. This stains the fingers red when you pick or prepare the shoots, but it comes off easily with *cold* water. Some people like the scorzonera roots more than those of salsify, once they learn not to peel them but to boil in the black skin which comes off more easily when rubbed in a cloth while still hot.

Prepare the ground for onions from seed, exactly as for sets, sowing in half-inch (1cm) deep furrows a foot (30cm) apart and thinning to six inches (15cm) between plants. They need the extra space to allow room for bending the foliage over to help ripening in July or August. If the stored onions run low, transplant some of the August-sown White Lisbon spring onions that should be ready to pull for salads now to six-inch (15 cm) each way spacing, and let them grow on to golf-ball size. They will not keep, but will fill the gap before the set grown onions are ripe. Those who have sown no spring onions can buy a bunch at a greengrocer's and plant them now. It is possible to snip the tips of the leaves off these repeatedly to add an onion taste to salads without spoiling the bulbs below – an example of eating your cake and having it, rare in gardening.

Parsley normally takes four to six weeks to germinate, and though it can be speeded up considerably by soaking it in urine overnight, it is best to sow radishes along the half-inch (1 cm) deep furrow for the single row which is all that is needed in view of the alkaloid, despite its excellent analysis. Hamburg parsley provides parsley-flavoured foliage – lower in the alkaloid – and roots. Sow the seeds in threes, eight inches (20 cm) apart and between rows, thinning to the best and keeping them hoed through the summer. They will be ready to dig in November and store or to leave in the ground all the winter, which gives the advantage of the foliage staying green for picking as a parsley substitute. The roots can be boiled or steamed like carrots or parsnips, which they rather resemble, or grated raw in salad. The large roots have the best flavour, so sow early on well-composted ground, with 4 oz a square yard (110 g a square metre) of fine bonemeal or blood, fish and bone before sowing if the soil is poor.

The reason unusual vegetables stay rare is because most gardeners leave them in too long while their wives wonder how to cook the strange monsters dumped in the kitchen. Kohl rabi is an unusual but useful vegetable, which looks like a turnip out of the ground and is in fact a kind of cabbage with a swollen stem for eating. It needs to be sown for succession, perhaps every four weeks – the last in June. Sow thinly first in March in half-inch (1 cm) deep furrows eight inches (20 cm) apart and thin to eight (20 cm) between plants, leaving the thinnings to grow about two inches (5 cm) tall, so they can be pulled to add their nutty flavour to salads. Ten weeks from sowing, their stem bulges should be rather smaller than cricket balls and ready to pull, cutting the leaves off for compost, for pulling breaks the skin and loses flavour. Do not peel; merely wash and boil like turnips. They can be eaten as ordinary turnips; sliced after boiling and fried with egg and breadcrumbs; diced to serve cold with mayonnaise, like potato salad, or grated raw. Alternatively, slice them into sticks and serve raw in glasses like a wholefood equivalent to potato crisps to eat with a clever but rather devious little home-made wine. The main value of kohl rabi lies in the high Vitamin A – 2500 IUs per 100g, or about sixteen times as much as cabbage and twenty-five times that of cauliflower, though they are not in the carrot class. The thinnings transplant well to the same spacing for a later batch from each sowing.

The autumn-sown lettuces will be starting to heart, and the value of having plenty is that they can be cut to fill a salad bowl when they are still only leaves. March is the time for the first outdoor sowings, but if plants from seed sown under glass early in February are available, they can be bought and planted out from the middle of the month when the weather turns more lamb-like. Take what you can get, with All the Year Round an old favourite of taste, and Cheshunt Early Ball and Lobjoit's Green Cos likely purchases to be ready in May.

Fortune is the fastest cabbage-type lettuce for March sowing thinly in half-inch (1cm) deep furrows eight inches (20cm) apart, thinning to eight inches (20cm) between plants staggered in the rows. Windermere, the finest frilly or 'crisp heart' variety needs spacing a foot (30cm) apart each way, with the same staggering, because they grow so large and last up to four weeks without bolting. Transplant some thinnings from each sowing to bring on a later batch and sow every six weeks rather than every four.

Little Gem, the tastiest of the cos varieties should be thinned to only six inches (15cm) because it is smaller, though it needs eight inches (20cm) between the rows to allow for hoeing, rubber banding to blanch them and selection. Winter Density, the best winter cos variety can also be sown in spring and summer for those who like a larger cos, spacing eight inches (20cm) each way.

Miner's lettuce and Lamb's-lettuce, otherwise known as 'corn salad', are the two odd men out among the natural orders which provide salads almost round the year for allergy sufferers. For normal gardeners they are useful hardy winter salads, far hardier than any lettuce, and can be grown every winter through frost and snow even in the most clubroot-haunted garden.

The best of the two is miner's lettuce, *Claytonia perfoliata*, (also known as 'winter purslane') named because it is found wild from Canada to California where the miners in the 1849 gold rush (and their 'daughters Clementine' for those who remember the old song) ate it as their only green food to go with salt pork, beans and 'dampers' of flour, fat and salt. It can be eaten for nine months of the year in Britain and in 1982 it throve under the snow as a far better source of Vitamin C than any expensive greenhouse lettuce. Analysed for the first time in January 1982 by the HDRA *Claytonia* showed 24mg per 100g compared with 3.4 for greenhouse lettuce, which is why it was so valuable in balancing a diet in which deer meat was the only fresh food.

The seeds are tiny, but keep for five years in the packet in an ordinary drawer, so there is no need to sow too thickly and 'use up the packet'. Mix the seed with about six times its bulk of fine bonemeal, which may be more expensive than fine sand but is about the same weight as small light seed, and sow it along the bottoms of half-inch (1cm) deep furrows the standard eight inches (20cm) apart. It is worth making white painted measuring sticks for the standard spacings to use with an ordinary garden line. Thin the seedlings to six inches (15cm) apart so they just meet in the rows when full sized, which, with this early sowing, will be by the end of May. In April the last of the winter crop runs to seed and there is a gap before the March sowing is ready to eat in June.

Lamb's lettuce, *Valerianella locusta*, was a weed of corn fields in Europe when 'corn' meant wheat, oats, rye and barley, as sold by corn-handlers, not as maize made into 'cornflakes' by Messrs Kellogg. It was fed to orphaned lambs by the farm-workers' wives who weeded wheat by hand when chemical weedkillers were still far in the future. This has the same pest and disease-dodging advantages as miner's lettuce, though without the crispness and neutral taste that makes it a food for every day like potatoes. The large-leafed type holds 57 mg per 100g of Vitamin C, which leaves greenhouse lettuce standing at the post in winter. Sow it mixed with bonemeal, like *Claytonia*, in March for a crop in May and June which can be cut off with scissors about half an inch (1 cm) above the neck to grow before the summer sowing in June is ready.

Landcress *(Barbarea praecox)* belongs to the cabbage tribe so can catch clubroot, and can only be eaten by allergy people on the same day as its fellow *Cruciferae* members, but it is very hardy, easy and holds the Vitamin C record for January with 82mg per 100g. It has almost exactly the taste of watercress and needs to be grown fast for it can be rather strong when it matures. Sow it first in March and the leaves will be ready to snip from its rosettes eight weeks later, as a new taste in summer salads.

Sow celery on Window-sills

Celery needs heat to start it, and it is often possible to buy young plants of Golden Self-Blanching to put out in mid-May, while the winter varieties can go out as late as June or July, fitting in after early potatoes. Celeriac, the turnip-rooted celery, is impossible to buy as a plant so it is worth raising some plants on a window-sill. Choose one that is really sunny, for light is more important for seedlings than heat, and save for this purpose the plastic containers in which rape or 'cress' is sold by greengrocers in winter, or other narrow trays that will stand in something to catch the surplus from waterings. The easiest soil you can obtain is John Innes Compost, sold in plastic bags from chainstores. This is not compost as known to organic gardeners, but a steam-sterilized potting soil. It will contain superphosphate as well as hoof and horn meal, but at such an early stage in the life of the crop it is not worth bothering about. Levington compost and other all-peat and chemical mixtures mean awkward watering. Purists should search for soil from molehills, which is fine, and pushed up from just below the soil under the turf. This will have weed seeds in it, but otherwise be entirely non-chemical.

Sow the celery and celeriac seed very thinly on the surface of the firmed and flattened soil, and fill the tray in which the containers stand with water so that it is sucked up and moistens the surface. Do this at intervals until the seedlings show celery-shaped leaves. Then transfer to other trays with more space, planting them about two inches (5cm) apart each way. March should be early enough to have them ready for June planting.

While you have seedlings growing on a sunny window-sill (where the celeriac will do the best because it needs less heat than celery), it is a good idea to raise also a herb that is not a hardy perennial. Basil *(Ocimum minimum)* can be sown in March, spaced out like celeriac and planted out in May, eight inches (20cm) apart, to grow on in a sunny border and ready to hang up to dry as soon as it flowers before storing in a screw-topped jar.

Garlic, too, should be planted as single cloves split from those bought from a greengrocer and planted two inches (5 cm) deep and six inches (15 cm) apart each way with the onions, to grow like sets and dry to store in the same way.

War on wireworms

The wireworm is the larva of the click beetle, of which *Agriotes lineatus* is the most common. It is between half and three-quarters of an inch (12-20mm) long at the pest stage, slender, light brown and with legs and jaws at one end. The adult beetles are no trouble, but in April, May and early June, the 'hens' lay about one hundred eggs each, usually in grass paths and lawns, or anywhere the ground stays undisturbed. At first the larvae are tiny and white, feeding on decayed vegetable matter and preyed on by so many predators that only 15 per cent reach the familiar wireworm size and spend up to four years eating potatoes and carrots, with the roots of leeks, onions, lettuce and tomatoes also popular. Peas and beans are less greedily eaten, though seeds that wait a long time ungerminated in a cold spring can be taken, but parsnips, kale and spinach usually escape.

Wireworms are pests of new gardens and allotments on old pasture land (which often holds eight million wireworms an acre) and neglected gardens. The best way to clear them is by green manuring with mustard. Rake the soil level and either scatter the seed at the rate of 2 oz a square yard (55g a square metre) and rake it in, or sow thinly along furrows six inches (15 cm) apart, between the end of March and early May. With an early start, the mustard will be eight inches (20cm) high, in bud (not flowering), and ready to dig under by the end of June, before the main July-October feeding period.

Old gardeners and farm-workers used to say that the wireworms fed so greedily on the mustard that they 'busted themselves'. We now know that wireworms spend from two to four years feeding according to the food available, and the mustard foliage 'finishes off' a record crop of beetles which will fly away and lay eggs where some modern farmer will slaughter them expensively with chemicals. A second sowing in July, dug in before the frost, will keep the wireworms eating the mustard rather than your crop. The mustard is of little value as a green manure because it is so soft and sappy.

This drastic counter-attack is not possible in the flower garden where wireworms attack bulbs, especially (it seems) the more expensive lilies, or where they are already doing the damage. They can be trapped during their two feeding periods – from March to mid-May and July to October. Cut some perforated zinc into pieces eight inches (20cm) long and six (15cm) wide, and bend these into cylinders two inches (5cm) in diameter. Lace them along the join with wire, flatten one end and lace this too, and make a wire handle at the other end. Set the traps by filling them with potato or carrot peelings and burying them upright in likely places. Pull them up by the handles every three or four days and dump the catch in the dustbin or chicken run.

The 'black wireworm' is the black millepede *(Tachypodjulus niger)* which coils like a fat watch spring if you pick it up, and feeds on potatoes, carrots and bulbs even more greedily. This creature is not going to change into anything and fly away, and the only defence is trapping; unfortunately it is too fat to get through the perforations in the zinc. Make traps out of tins, fitting these over the end of a stout, round post, and jab holes in

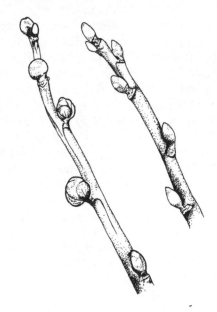

5 Blackcurrrant shoots – normal (right) and infected by big-bud mites, *Eriophyes ribis*, (left).

the bottom and sides with an old-fashioned tin-opener, or use a power drill with a three-sixteenth-inch bit (or its modern decimal equivalent). Determined trapping round the year will banish these pests, and only the chickens will miss them.

Fruit care in March
From mid-March to mid-April is the only time to catch the big-bud mite of blackcurrants *(Cecidophyopsis ribis)* out without its 'big bud' on, for it is then that this tiny pest that carries the reversion virus is migrating from the swollen buds which should be picked off whenever they are seen. They can be spread from bush to bush by clothes, they blow on the wind, and even hitch-hike rides on birds. Spray with a derris insecticide when the leaves are the size of 5p pieces, which will spare the *Anthocoris* bugs as they do their best to control the mites.

The currant aphid *(Cryptomyzus galeopsidis)* which curls the leaves at the tips, making it difficult to kill by spraying, can be caught with nicotine in February or March before the leaves are open to protect it.

7.

April

Available for eating	Family	Sowing	Planting
Artichokes, Jerusalem	3	–	February-March
Beans (dried or frozen)	7	May-June	–
Beet (stored)	2	May	–
Broccoli (late sprouting)	4	April	June
Cabbage	4	June	July
Carrots (stored)	12	May	–
Celery	12	March-April	May-June
Kale	4	April	June-July
Leeks	8	April	July
Lettuce (winter)	3	August-September	–
Onions (spring)	8	August	–
Onions (stored)	8	March	–
Peas (dried or frozen)	7	January-May	–
Potatoes (stored)	11	–	April-May
Radish, Chinese	4	July	–
Rhubarb	9	April	February
Salsify (leaves)	3	April	–
Spinach (winter)	2	September	–
Sweetcorn (frozen)	6	April-May	–
Tomatoes (bottled)	11	–	May-June

Potato planting

In the south, early potatoes can be sneaked out early in March, but this risks their coming through too soon and getting caught by late frosts. It is better to dig in a green-manure crop or compost and manure first and wait till April with the seed still safe in its chitting trays. On light soils, the quickest and easiest way to plant potatoes is to make seven-inch (18cm) deep holes with a steel-shod dibber along a garden line, a foot (30cm) apart and eighteen inches (45cm) between rows for earlies and fifteen inches (38cm) apart and twenty-seven (68cm) between rows for maincrop. Then drop the seed tubers down the holes (rose end up) and dibber the soil back over them.

The disadvantage of this method of planting is that it is impossible to place the manure or compost where it will do most good, and on clay soils the dibber puddles the sides till the hole can hold water and either rot the tuber or give it a slow start. Trenching is harder work but as the potatoes are rotated round the garden every bed will have had the benefit of deep digging and deep manuring. It is easy to dig down and find where last year's trenches were and have them in a new place each season.

Dig the trenches nine inches (23cm) wide and a foot (30cm) deep to allow room for well-rotted manure or compost on the bottom. This can be the part-rotted surface layers, or any compost that has not heated well, because at this depth weed seeds do no harm. On chalky or sandy soils a layer of leaf-mould on the bottom is an asset to retain moisture. With seed safely chitting it is possible to let the maincrops wait until the first cut of comfrey is ready; leave this to wilt overnight to concentrate, and put 1½-2lb (650-900g) of wilted comfrey to the foot (30cm) of row, with lawn-mowings in addition, to tread into a four-inch (10cm) thick layer.

Whatever method is used, add two inches (5cm) of soil on top, then set out the seed potatoes, eye up, along it, and fill in with the soil from the next trench. Comfrey alone, or with grass, decays in a kind of long, narrow 'compost heap', releasing plant foods, but also producing humic acids. Potato scab *(Streptomyces scabies)*, unlike clubroot, *likes* a limey soil, and the acidity from decay protects the potatoes which stay in the trench. On chalk, where scab is worst, or where heavy liming has been used against clubroot, make the trenches a foot (30cm) wide and deep and use leaf-mould generously (but not last autumn's leaves – they should be the previous autumn's crop).

An intermediate method in terms of work is to dig the bed deeply to the full depth of the fork, leaving a long, straight trench, put three inches (8cm) of compost, manure, or comfrey along it, add about an inch (2.5cm) of soil and then set out the seed. Pile the soil from the next trench on top and dig till the next straight trench comes at the right spacing. This leaves ridges along the planted potato rows, and it has the advantage that seaweed meal at the rate of 4 oz a square yard (110g a square metre) or rock potash at 8 oz a square yard (220g a square metre) can be dug in at the same time.

If the potatoes come through during a frosty period, draw soil over them with the hoe, or go out after the TV weather forecast and spread newspapers over them, weighed down with canes (for if frost threatens, it will not be windy). When the shoots are six inches (15cm) high and the weeds are starting to grow, draw the soil towards the shoot rows with a swan-neck hoe, the operation known as 'earthing up', which should be done in three stages so you get three kills of seedling weeds before the haulm spreads and takes over weed control. This is why potatoes are called a 'clearing crop'.

Vegetables sowings and care in April

April is the time to sow the slow-maturing cabbage-tribe crops for transplanting. This is best done in a separate seedbed because they are going to fit in after the pea-tribe crops which, especially any for drying, will need their room up to the last minute. The seedbed need not be in full sun, though this is best, but it must be possible to water it, and it needs 2 lb a square yard (900g a square metre) of lime every other year, holding it at pH 8.5 if you have a soil tester. A good rotation for this bed would be seedlings followed by radishes, summer and winter and drying beans the following season, for the pea tribe love lime, too.

Sow early and late sprouting broccoli, summer cauliflowers, winter cauliflowers (once called 'heading broccoli'), Brussels sprouts, cabbages (summer and winter), and kale, formerly called 'borecole'. Sow all the earlier varieties now, leaving savoys, late-winter and spring cabbages such as April for May sowing. The furrows should be eight inches (20cm) apart, and thin sowing is essential, aiming at two inches (5cm) between seeds – not only for economy, because cabbage-tribe seed will keep at least five years, but because uncrowded seedlings make the best plants. Quarter of an ounce (7g) of any of these mean 2,000 seeds, and most gardeners sow 500 when they want at most fifty.

The seedbed should ideally be large enough to act as a holding area for the Brussels sprouts impatiently waiting for the peas to finish. When the seedlings are three inches (8 cm) high, dig them up, snip the tip off the root to make them grow a web of side roots, rather than a single thin taproot, and plant them four inches (10 cm) apart each way to wait for moving to their final homes.

The major pest of the cabbage tribe is the cabbage-root fly *(Delia brassicae)* and the first hatch from their pupae in the soil is in late April and early May. They hunt by scent and the best way to make sure that the seedlings in the rows or the waiting bed do not have maggots in their roots is to thrust in a six-foot (2m) bamboo cane in the middle of the bed and hang a strip of old blanket from it. Then paint a streak of creosote down the blanket, a decoy scent which has been used successfully by organic market gardeners. There are two more hatches, late June to mid-July and August to September, and other measures are needed once the crop is beyond the seedling stage.

The best counter-measure is to cut eight-inch (20 cm) squares of roofing felt, carpet or carpet underlay, with a slit running in to the centre where it is widened to fit the stem. These can be fitted round the cabbages as soon as they are planted, and care should be taken to see they sit flat on the ground and hide the soil: the fly is programmed to lay its eggs just where the stem joins the ground, and this is why even thick polythene is useless. The last hatch of flies can lay eggs on the foliage where they bore into the stems and destroy winter cabbage just when the price is highest. The Scots market gardener who found the creosote trick has bamboo canes and creosoted blanket strips spaced at twenty feet (6-7m) intervals each way on a four-acre field, as the cheapest scent masker.

Leeks are ready to sow in April so that strong plants are ready to fit in behind the first early potatoes, which are dug as soon as they are in full flower. They do not mind ample lime, so they can be sown with the cabbages in the seedbed, aiming at an inch (2.5 cm) between the quite large seeds. Those who want to eat leeks in September and November can sow a fast kind like Early Market, while a slow one to outlast Musselbugh is Sutton's Winter Crop to extend the season until the end of April. Though leeks and onions are a useful source of sulphur, their main dietary value is the Vitamin A in the leaves, so merely shorten these to half length instead of trimming away the best part as greengrocers will.

Spinach family problem

The taste of spinach comes from oxalic acid, and though New Zealand spinach is in a natural order all on its own, it has about a third as much as the summer spinach in the shoot tips which are eaten. It has the advantage of supplying spinach all the summer without the constant resowing that summer spinach needs to keep up a supply. New Zealand spinach *(Tetragonia expansa)* can be sown in the open in April, or May in the north. It is slow to germinate, so should be soaked in cold water overnight and sown in threes, spaced a foot (30cm) apart each way, and thinned to the best in each cluster when all are up and thriving.

Start picking when the sprawling, fleshy, shoots are six inches (15cm) long, and take about three inches (8cm) of stem and dark-green arrowhead leaves from each, and keep on picking from June until the frosts kill it. It will seed itself from the insignificant flowers along the stems, and it pays to leave it to grow of its own accord every year. It is tastiest when constantly picked, and if a guesthouse or nature clinic could keep on top of the production of one twelve-foot (4m) row, the yield would be fantastic.

The best of the spinach family is Swiss chard, a beet grown for its leaves and which has wide, heavy midribs, sometimes cooked separately, that can be four inches (10cm) wide. There are a number of varieties of which Lucullus is the hardiest green, and Ruby or Rhubarb, a striking red and a favourite with flower arrangers. Sow in April or May in clusters of three (thinned to the best) a foot (30cm) apart with fifteen inches (38cm) between rows to allow room for walking between and twisting off the leaves that can be eighteen inches (45cm) long, as well as hoeing. These are for summer cating.

Spinach beet, or perpetual spinach, will also produce a supply of green food from July into the autumn, even right round until April from an August sowing. Sow the large seeds in pairs a foot (30cm) apart in inch-deep (2.5cm) dibber holes with fifteen inches (38cm) between rows. Pick the leaves by bending them down until they break off, not cutting or pulling in case they bleed. Cut off any flower stems that grow in summer and never strip a plant – sow plenty to share the burden. Summer spinach, if required for salads, should be sown at three-week intervals from March until the last in September, each sowing taking about five weeks to grow from seed and offering three weeks' picking before it bolts.

Table 13: Comparative levels of oxalic acid in long-season vegetables

	Calcium %	Oxalic acid %
Chenopodium album		
(the weed fat-hen)	0.0990	1.1100
young leaves	–	0.052
Spinach, ordinary	0.1330	0.8920
Beet leaves	0.1200	0.9160
New Zealand spinach (leaves)	0.1100	0.8900
Seakale beet (chard) leaves	0.1100	0.6600
Seakale beet (chard) midribs	0.0450	0.2900
New Zealand spinach (stems)	0.0830	0.6500
New Zealand spinach (tips)	–	0.3400
Parsley	0.2900	0.1900
Beetroot (unpeeled)	0.0180	0.1380
Broccoli	0.2100	0.0054
Kale	0.3100	0.0130
Cabbage	0.1890	0.0077
Carrots	0.0440	0.0330
Lettuce	0.0730	0.0071
Rhubarb (cooked stems)	0.0440	0.5000

The problem of these useful, long-season vegetables, with hardly any pests or diseases, is their oxalic acid level shown in Table 13. Unfortunately, breeding for a low oxalic acid level, when this is what they are intentionally grown for, is as unrewarding as designing a silent transistor radio. Rhubarb leaves are so high in oxalic acid that there have been poisoning cases, but there has never been a case of spinach poisoning, and only vegans, or those on a milk-free or other low-calcium diet, risk shortage. On the other hand, it would be risky to live entirely on beet leaves. In 1948, refugees in Dresden, Berlin and Leipzig were treated in hospital for oxalic poisoning and liver damage from excessive Vitamin A, after living for several weeks on cooked *Chenopodium album* growing on the rubble of bombed buildings. The answer is to eat beet roots and not leaves and not to make anything your sole diet.

Nutritionally this group of vegetables is valuable, as shown in Table 14, but in vegetables Vitamin A is present as Carotene, which is converted by the liver into the vitamin. In the case of *Chenopodium* beet leaves and spinach, this is far higher even than in carrots, and can be a great strain on the liver. A fashion for beet-leaf eating, like glue sniffing, would be a serious health risk. Young *Chenopodium* leaves gathered in the spring, however, have little more oxalic acid than kale.

Table 14: Nutritional composition of long-season vegetables

	A (IUs)	C	E	Niacin	Thiamine	Riboflavin
			Mg per 100g		µg per 100g	
Spinach, ordinary	8,400-25,000	59-75	1.70	0.70 0.20	50,120	240-300
Spinach, New Zealand	1,400	62.50	0.20	1–1	1–1	1–1
Chenopodium	19,000	85	1.80	1.00	59	690
Beet leaves	21,000	34-50	1–1	0.30	50	170-300
Carrots	10,000	6-10	1–1	1.50	60-70	60
Kale	7,000-20,000	100	8.00	0.80	120	350-500

Sweetcorns and pumpkins

In our climate, we can grow sweetcorn for eating on the cob if we choose a fast kind like Sutton's First of All. We can enjoy it freshly picked from the end of August, and then from the deep freeze, and the bulk of compost material it grows is a welcome bonus. Sweetcorn, or maize, is greedy for phosphorus, and purple streaks on the leaves are the sign of shortage. Sweetcorn is a pleasant rest for a cabbage-weary soil, but do look over the bed in April for any seedlings of *Chenopodium*, not only to eat when it is young and tasty, but to see if it is pink or even pale, red-purple round the growing point. This is a certain sign of phosphorus shortage and it is also worth checking a new strawberry bed before planting, for strawberries also demand phosphorus. If dried sewage sludge is available, spread 8 oz a square yard (220g a square metre) before digging ready for sowing, and if not scatter 8 oz (220g) of fine bonemeal instead.

Sow the large seeds an inch (2.5cm) deep, making a depression with the trowel to hold water, fifteen inches (38cm) apart and two feet (60cm) between rows, then cover each with a

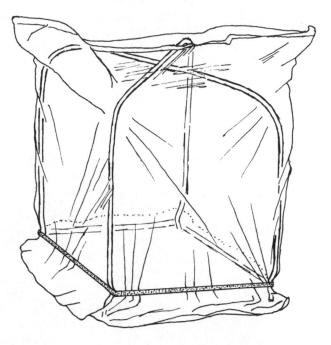

6 Polythene-bag 'cloche' for pumpkins and cucumbers

polythene bag 'cloche'. These are made with two eighteen-inch (45 cm) lengths of 20-gauge galvanized iron wire, bent into a giant hairpin about four inches (10 cm) wide; thrust the ends of the wires into the ground across the seed so it makes a 'croquet hoop' about four inches (10 cm) high, and set the other one across it. Pull a small polythene bag down over the hoops with a rubber band round the bottom to prevent it blowing away. Water the depression under the 'cloche' and, because the sun on the polythene will warm the weeds ahead as well as the corn, after two weeks remove the bags, weed and inspect your corn. When the shoot is three inches (8 cm) long, remove the bags and wires and let the corn grow, storing the bags and wires for the next season. Sweetcorn can be sown in May without cloches, but it gains from the flying start.

Polythene-bag cloches give the same gain in growing time for pumpkins, marrows, courgettes and outdoor cucumbers, which can also be sown in March if there is room on a sunny window-sill and the care and attention to keep them watered in their plastic pots of John Innes compost. Plant these out in mid-

April, but protect them from frosts and cold winds for the first few nights by spreading a cardboard carton over each, with its flaps spread and weighed down with stones.

Pumpkins have shoots that race for long distances and they will not fit into a neat rotation. They should go on rough ground that needs something to cover it and that will hold down weeds. Dig holes five feet (1 m50) apart each way, and a foot (30 cm) square and deep. Fill these half full of trodden, rough compost or leaf-mould and kitchen waste, topped with replaced soil packed down to leave an inch-deep (2.5 cm) depression round each, which can be filled with water by hose if the pumpkins flag in drought. Take off the cartons when the weather is friendly and let the pumpkins run. When each shoot has grown at least one plain stemmed male flower and one female, with a miniature round pumpkin behind it, cut the shoot off after this female flower. If such trimming can be kept up this should mean more moderate-sized pumpkins to store and fewer monsters for weight guessing in aid of Oxfam.

Modern outdoor cucumbers are far nicer than the old rough skinned type. Grow them on the same system, but with holes only three feet (1 m) apart each way, remembering, however, that unlike the pumpkins, they cannot be stored for winter use. This applies also to marrows and courgettes, both as bush types for the three-foot (1 m) spacing. Marrows can be left to grow woody by those who want to make marrow jam, but if they are allowed to mature like pumpkins they will keep, but they can no longer be cooked as a vegetable. Courgettes need picking every day, and if you can keep pace with them they are good value for space, but not in food for, like cucumbers, they are mostly water.

The radishes between the parsnips will have finished and as they take about twenty days from seed to salad, sowing thinly in pairs of furrows two inches (5 cm) apart about every three weeks will keep up the supply. Radishes are in and out of the soil so fast they escape clubroot and can fit in like extra sowings of lettuce wherever there is room. A second sowing of early peas should go in now, early, because the maincrops need high and costly sticks but anything only eighteen inches (45 cm) or two feet (60 cm) tall can be cheaply supported.

It is possible to cut relatively short branching sticks in the country and it is far easier to thrust them in along the rows than to find anything taller than two feet (60 cm). Stout nylon net can be bought up to this height, and wire netting about two feet (60cm) tall stretched round posts at the end of the rows, and held upright by canes thrust down the sides, doubles as support and protection from birds for peas that have outgrown their guards. The netting lasts for years if it is unhooked and rolled up to store in a shed at the end of the season.

Pest control in April

Peas in some gardens develop 'scalloped edges' to the new leaves, caused by the pea weevil. Water along the rows with the cigarette-end nicotine solution diluted one part to two of cold water, using a rosed can to soak the surface. This should catch the weevils when they come out at night, and be spent in forty-eight hours.

The safest pesticide of all – which spares both bees and ladybirds, and their larvae – for aphids and small caterpillars, but not strong enough for weevils, is quassia, which is chips of wood of *Picrasma quassioides.* Simmer 4 oz in a gallon (110g in 4.5 litres) of water for an hour, topping up as it boils away; pour off the yellow liquid when cool and dilute with five parts of water for aphids and three for caterpillars. This can be safely sprayed on the gooseberry sawfly caterpillars *(Nematus ribesii)* which can strip a bush in four days. When mature they fall to the ground, pupate for a few days and start successive broods every five weeks in summer. Watch for the small, green or blue-green caterpillars on the leaves in April and May, at first attacking only the surface, then boring holes right through, and catch them with quassia.

Anthocoris is the natural controller of gooseberry mite *(Bryobia praetiosa)* which attacks in April and May in hot, dry weather, turning the leaves grey with the loss of sap so that they drop early and starve the fruit. Spray with quassia, which does not harm Anthocoris, getting it well under the leaves, or use the paraffin emulsion, made up with toilet paraffin, which is more expensive but quickly available from any chemist.

In April a number of caterpillars are just starting in the orchard, and the safest counter-measure is a 2 per cent nicotine-and-soap wash, which can be bought ready-made. It is quickly spent, spares Anthocoris and ladybirds, and if sprayed on in the evenings will have lost much of its danger by the time the bees are at work again. Spray against apple capsid *(Haplocampa testudinea)* before the blossom buds open and after the petals have fallen with the quassia for apple sawfly. Strawberry aphis *(Myzus fragariella)* starts in April and spraying with nicotine and soap will catch the 'stem mothers' from eggs before they spread and swarm, carrying the virus diseases of strawberries.

It is no longer necessary to smear sticky material on to greaseproof-paper bands and tie them round the trees, for modern greases can be safely painted on the bark, and there is no risk that determined wingless female winter moths *(Cheimatobis brumata)* will find a subway under it along a hollow in the trunk, for older trees may not be perfectly round. Inspect the grease to make sure no twig or leaf has blown against it and stuck to form a bridge, and renew the mixture to stop the summer traffic up your trees.

8.

May

Available for eating	Family	Sowing	Planting
Beans (dried or frozen)	7	May-June	–
Beet (stored)	2	May	–
Broccoli (late sprouting)	4	April	June
Cabbage	4	June	July
Carrots (stored)	12	May	–
Kale	4	April	June-July
Leeks	8	April	July
Lettuce (winter)	3	August-September	–
Onions (spring)	8	August	–
Onions (stored)	8	March	–
Peas (dried or frozen)	7	January-May	–
Potatoes (stored)	11	–	April-May
Radishes	4	March-August	–
Rhubarb	9	April	February
Spinach (summer)	2	February	–
Sweetcorn (frozen)	6	April-May	–
Tomatoes (bottled)	11	–	May-June

Tomato plant time

Once it was possible to buy tomato plants raised in heat with a choice of varieties, but the loss of the passenger-train parcels service forces us to take whatever the local garden centre sells, or to grow our own. Harbinger, the best early ripener with a thin skin and a real taste can be raised on a window-sill, in a box of

John Innes seed soil, covered with a sheet of glass turned every morning to take away the condensation, and removed when the seedlings appear. Pot them, when real tomato leaves show between the two pointed seed leaves, and keep them growing on the window-sill till about the second week in May. The plants will be smaller than bought ones, about six inches (15 cm) high, but commercial plants are grown to greenhouse planting size, which is on the large side for outdoors.

Some gardens have a single sunny border where the tomatoes must go each year, and this can be rotated with cucumbers and runner beans, with a green manure crop sown each winter and dug in each spring. The best policy is to rotate them round with the vegetables, ideally following the sprouting broccoli which come out as they go in.

Dig holes for the plants, like those for pumpkins, two feet (60 cm) apart and three (1 m) between rows to allow room for trimming, tying and picking. Put two inches (5 cm) of leaf-mould on the bottom of the hole, add four inches (10 cm) of compost and fill up with soil, threading these firm and leaving a half-inch (1 cm) deep depression on top. This will deepen as the compost and leaf-mould sink, but as tomatoes grow larger they will need to trap water from can or hose. Drive in a stake in the centre of each hole because if it goes in when the plants are large and waiting for it, this may damage the roots.

Ideally, you need a five-foot (1 m50) dahlia stake, for it must stand about four feet (1 m20) above ground, but height is expensive these days. Reject broom-handles can sometimes be bought; dahlia stakes are good but expensive, and ordinary 1 x 1 inch (2.5 cm) timber, pointed and sawn to size is cheaper. It is essential to coat any stake with creosote or other wood preservative, because the watering means that bare wood rots at ground level and soon your stakes are too short to use.

Put out the plants, taking care not to break the soil ball, water well, then open out a colour supplement magazine and secure it to the stake with drawing pins. This will keep the wind off the plant and protect it from frost for the first week after planting, but should be burnt or thrown in the dustbin when the plants are safe in the open, because glazed paper composts badly and has toxic metals in its ink, though supplements last better in the open than popular periodicals of the same size. Tie a short length of non-nylon string first round the stake and then round the young plant as a first support.

Celery and celeriac

Self-blanching celery for the summer needs no trenches. Spread a bucketful of compost to the square yard or metre and dig over the bed before spacing out the bought or window-sill-raised plants, a foot (30cm) apart and eighteen inches (45cm) between rows, making a depression round each to hold water, both to start them and for when they need watering in drought. Ordinary celery can be planted in May, but as it is demanding in space it can wait till late June or July when the early potatoes come out and release room.

By mid-May, each of the seedling celeriac should have a slight bulge at the base ready to earn it the name of 'turnip-rooted celery'. Plant them like the Golden Self-Blanching celery with the bulge at ground level and give them a well-watered start. Hoe them, like the celery, and their stem bases will swell on the surface until they look like turnips with celery tops. Remove any sideshoots that appear and by October they can weigh as much as 3 lb (1.3kg) each. Grate them raw in salads through the winter and treat them like kohl rabi, the other swollen-stem vegetable that is also unappreciated. They can be lifted, the tops removed, and then stored as root vegetables, but it is better to earth them up with mature leaf-mould as a winter protection.

May is a better time to sow beet for winter storage than March; June is not too late, but the May sowing brings the cricket-ball sizes that keep well and give a worthwhile supply of food from the space. Chantenay Red Cored carrots, or Sutton's Favourite (a larger form of Chantenay) for winter storage are also best sown at the same spacing as the earlies, but towards the end of this month. This sowing will be ready for thinning when the first carrot-fly attack is over, but it may suffer from the August and September onslaught.

Countering carrot-fly

The carrot-fly *(Psila rosae)*, belongs to the same family as the cabbage-root fly, and the traditional remedies rely on masking this scent with something stronger. Planting carrots next to onions, scattering lawn-mowings between the rows at fortnightly intervals to maintain a barrage of hay scent, soaking sawdust in paraffin and sprinkling it along the rows and winding string round short stakes, dipping this in creosote and thrusting them in at intervals, all have their advocates confident of success, but they also have their failures.

They probably are effective on carrot-flies homing in on the thinnings from the maximum range of seven miles, five miles or even a mile, but when the pupae are hatching in the garden next door, the flies use their eyes. One new and quite effective method developed on the HDRA Trial Ground is to surround a three-foot (1m) wide and twelve foot (4m) long carrot bed with clear polythene, ideally 16-inch (40cm) wide tubing with a string along the top and bottom edges to stretch it firmly round four stout corner posts. Stapling over the string rather than the polythene prevents the wind tearing it away. The treated plots inside the polythene curtain gave a 47 per cent yield increase compared with the plots without polythene which had 29.2 per cent carrot-fly-damaged roots compared with 10.8 per cent for the protected plots.

The increase in yield was because of the sheltering 'greenhouse effect' from the polythene, but quite a proportion of the flies were evidently coming in along the bed instead of across. Tall tins with tops and bottoms removed, bitumen painted, would be cheaper and could be more effective. The commercial carrot growers hire fields or suitable soil for a single season and move to another seven miles off before the flies arrive and build up. They fly along the headlands, feeding on the nectar and pollen of hemlock and cow-parsley; spraying these with Aldrin and other organo-chlorine compounds has exterminated the natural enemies of the pests and produced resistant strains of all these awkward flies. Those who are really interested, and have gardens or farms infested with carrot, cabbage or onion flies should write to the HDRA for the latest news on the battle to find an organic answer to a problem that has no good *inorganic* one either.

Sow drying peas in May

The tall but early Pilot peas for drying, with White Achievement and any other runner beans to pick green or dry, should be sown or planted in May. It is possible to steal a march on the year by sowing the peas singly in pots or yoghurt cartons with half-inch (1cm) holes melted in the bottoms and set on sand in watertight trays on window-sills, to plant out in May from March sowings. Runner beans are more robust, and setting out the seeds, two inches (5cm) apart each way in a tray full of leaf-mould, in March and keeping them watered on a window-sill allows them to be planted in May rather than sown. The cost of a small greenhouse or even a frame is so high today that, in view of the fact that it is only of value for three months – February, March and April, the gain in time and crop is not enough to balance the cost and trouble of the many plastic substitutes for pots and seedtrays and the heating and upkeep. Window-sills win!

The best support for Pilot is metre-wide wire netting (the wider the mesh the cheaper), supported on stout stakes at each row end, like those of normal peas. Because they will not be picked, the rows can be eighteen (45 cm) instead of thirty inches (75 cm) apart, which still allows space for hoeing. Pick some of the lower pods for eating but when the leaves start yellowing and the oldest pods wrinkle and split, withhold water and let them dry slowly. When the lowest pods gape it is time to pull up the stakes, cut off the stems at ground level, lay them on polythene in the sun to ripen, beat them with a stick when the pods are crisp and pull the haulm off the netting for compost. The peas for eating in soups and stew through the winter can be stored in polythene sweet-jars or anything airtight, but those for next year's seed should go into paper envelopes in a dry drawer because they need to breathe. Drying your own peas is an unfashionable art, and therefore it is no longer possible to buy such old drying varieties as Harrison's Glory through seedsmen. The way round the regulations is to buy from a supermarket a packet of dry green peas, which will probably be Maro, Proco or Alaska only sold on contract to farmers, and sow it in March, April or May. It will be a heavier crop but not as fast as Pilot, and may well be tastier for it was bred to hold its flavour when dried.

Sugar peas should be gathered young to eat pods and all, but they are better still when grown to pick for raw eating in salads. They are extra sweet, and contain about five times the amount of Vitamin C, three times the riboflavin, and four times as much thiamine as those bought canned or frozen. Because they grow tall, they need netting like Pilot.

Beans in May
Runner beans are taller still and need eight-foot (2m50) bamboo canes, set out as in the illustration. Using pairs of canes in inverted 'V's every four feet (1m20), instead of every eight inches (20cm), and filling in with strings led down to metal skewers from the cross-canes at the top, saves money, for string

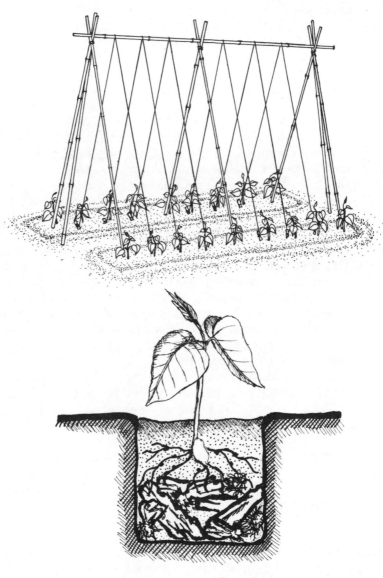

Smashed cabbage stumps and Brussels sprout stems

7 Bean trench

is cheaper. The canes should spread about a foot (30cm) at the bottom, and the beans be sown or planted in a double row along the sides of the foot-wide (30cm) trench. Few families need more than a single twelve-foot (4m) row of runners, because the yield depends on how closely they are picked. Take the large, low pods first and just pick and pick for eating and freezing from even a dozen plants.

Drying beans are grown in the same way, but without picking, and as they run higher and flop over above the canes, cut the upper growth and small pods with the shears for compost material to put more strength into the driers. These should be picked when they are light brown and split easily, ready to set out in the potato chitting trays which are stacked on top of each other to finish drying. Another way to grow drying beans is from vine-eyes (like big screw-eyes in rawlplugs) as high up the side of the house as your steps will reach, or you can twist one into a bedroom window-sill. Runner beans were originally imported as ornamental climbers for Chatsworth-size greenhouses, and they are twiners round strings, rather than tendril clingers like peas. So they will go fifteen or even twenty feet (5-6m) up strings held down by metal skewers in a rubbish-filled bean-trench below a windowless wall. If you have two suitable positions, alternate them with *Tropaeolum peregrinum*, the bright yellow-flowered Canary creeper, or *Ipomaea purpurea*, the hardiest of the Morning Glories, as two good, climbing, hardy annuals which will offer a mass of compost material when the strings are cut in the autumn; the beans offer all this and food too. The best runner bean for drying is the Czar, which has white flowers and seeds exactly like rather smaller butter beans, but with a nicer flavour than any on sale in packets today. Second choice is White Achievement, a climbing french bean which produces haricot sizes.

French beans

French beans have only the family and the deep freeze to keep pace with, so you need fewer than you think. Start picking when the pods are only four inches long and never let them grow large and yellow, for then they cease production and ripen what they have. Their trenches should be eight inches (20cm) apart, and the beans go six inches (15cm) apart and two inches (5cm) deep.

Purley King is the best drier, with Romano runner up.

Horsehead, the best of all, has hit EEC trouble, because the patent fees cripple a variety that has been bred for the relatively few people who want to dry their own. The seed trade is now where publishing would be if books were taxed, with the same rate for bestsellers as first volumes of poems, and no firm would print anything but TV linked works to sell millions. We may yet come to this.

Drying French beans is easiest of all. Just tie them to a short stake to keep them upright and the heavy pods clear of the ground until the pods yellow and split. Uproot them and hang heads down in a dry shed to ripen, then spread on a polythene bag and beat with a stick till the pods split. If there is time they can be picked as they ripen and set out to dry in the chitting trays like the butter beans.

It is not possible to grow soya beans for successful drying in Britain, for we have summers entirely unlike those of China, Japan, Canada, USA or Sweden. It is not frosts that matter but the lack of a long, dry, autumn or 'Indian summer', with longer days from closer proximity to the Arctic Circle. Though the amino-acid balance of soya beans is excellent, the hairy, two-seeded pods are no better nutritionally than French beans if they are eaten green, and give a fraction of the crop.

Those who would like to dry a bean for concentrated protein can grow daffa beans, the field beans with a yield of 1½ tons an acre, used to make British 'textured vegetable protein'. The daffa bean is a relation of the broad bean, but without the awkward alkaloid that makes this poisonous if eaten raw and prevents it being used for drying, and with more but smaller pods that point upwards instead of out. Sow them two inches (5cm) deep, six inches (15cm) apart and a foot (30cm) between rows in October or November, to harvest in August when the pods turn black and split. They need hoeing once or twice to keep the weeds down and, like broad beans, need their growing points taken out in late May or early June with about three inches (8cm) of soft stem, which is where the black fly *(Aphis fabae)* attacks.

Cut the plants at ground level, let them dry in a shed and beat them between plastic bags with a stick, then sift out the beans – quicker than shelling them individually. Like all dried beans, they should be soaked before cooking and though not very tasty they are nicer than soya beans.

Sow the second batch of cabbage-tribe plants towards the

end of the month, extra lettuces and another batch of lamb's-lettuce and miner's lettuce for those who must have constant changes in their salads. Keep up the lettuce sowings, thinning and transplanting to stretch each one over six weeks. Watch for small holes in radish and cabbage plant seedlings, which will be caused by the flea beetle, small, black and skipping, for which derris dust is the best answer.

Organic fruit care in May

In May, the apple capsid *(Plesiocoris rugicollis)* and the green capsid *(Lygus pabulinus)* – tubby little bugs about quarter-of-an-inch (7mm) long – may be seen running about leaves on sunny days in May and June. They are quite distinct from aphids because they are faster, larger and greedier. The answer for the apple capsids, which suck the leaves surrounding the blossom so that the fruitlets develop corky patches, is to hose the trees, squirting the water up high and hard. The disturbance shakes the capsids down as rain rarely does, and as they are wingless they get caught on the grease-band round the trunk, renewed in April.

The green capsid attacks gooseberries, currants, raspberries and roses, but unfortunately these cannot be grease-banded. Paint two lengths of hardboard about a foot (30cm) wide and a yard (1m) long with the grease-band material, slide these one on each side of the gooseberry, currant or rose bush, and either shake the bush or hose or syringe with force. The grease is water-proof and the boards may last another season, if protected with other sheets of hardboard, but separated by nailing strips of wood round the sides and ends. The raspberry beetle is out laying eggs in the blossom on sunny days in May and June and to spray with anything strong enough to kill a beetle means killing bees. The dig-over trick is one way round, but another is to set the greased boards on each side of the row, on a dull day when the beetles will not be flying but resting and crawling, and shake the canes so they fall on to the grease. Two people sliding the boards along and shaking can go over a raspberry bed almost as fast as if they were spraying with something deadly.

The raspberry weevil *(Otiorhyncus picipes)* is nocturnal and the best control is to go out with the boards at night and shine a powerful torch along the canes to deceive the weevils into thinking it is time to drop quickly and to go home to bed under clods or in a mulch. This creature, sometimes called the 'clay-

coloured weevil', also attacks gooseberries, apples, damsons
and strawberries, eating young blossom and leaves as well as
attacking the bark on young shoots. In orchards switch on the
light of a large torch *suddenly*. Spread newspapers if you want
to hear them patter down, but coating these with grease is too
time-consuming and costly, and entirely unnecessary; the
weevils are wingless and are caught by the grease bands, which
can have the surface scraped off and given a fresh coat if there is
a bad weevil epidemic (they are rumoured to be producing
organo-chlorine resistant varieties).

It is not possible to grease-band raspberries, so spray with
nicotine soap wash, *but do not pick any raspberries for
seventy-two hours* to make sure that it has become harmless
There are a number of other weevils that can be controlled in the
same way, and there is no need to bother about the names, for if
anything is walking about in your trees at night it is up to no
good. Anthocoris mites are not nocturnal and cling on tighter in
bark crevices; the adults are winged and can fly back. Some
weevils fly, but reluctantly, for they are rather under-engined
for their weight.

There is no room in this book to describe these pests and their
life cycles, only the organic remedies where these exist. The
scientific names are given so that descriptions can be checked in
standard reference works from libraries. They may be off-
putting for beginners, but there is no law of nature that says
beginners only get pests with simple answers and easy names.

In the past chickens were kept in orchards partly as pest
eaters. Work at East Malling in the 1940s showed that chickens
are less efficient than ducks. The newly popular Welsh
Harlequin breed, which lays eggs with white 'whites' almost
identical with hens' eggs, are the best slug-eaters of all. Protect
seedlings with wire pea-guards and let the ducks roam the
gardens. Perhaps someone will breed a nocturnal strain of this
old Welsh duck which has been scavenging slugs ever since the
Welsh had two 'L's to rub together.

Geese graze orchards, and too many of them will eat
everything but the plantains, but they are grazing birds and not
of value as pest controllers. Ducks and chickens (especially
bantams, which offer more beaks and keen pairs of eyes to the
pound of supplementary food) are at their most valuable
between the beginning of May and the end of September. There
would be scope for an organic poultry farmer to run the flock on

deep litter or straw yard with artificial lighting from September till April, and in an old-fashioned wheeled house moved occasionally in an orchard. This would increase the tiny total of *genuine* free-range eggs sold in Britain today.

The lackey moth has hairy caterpillars up to 1½ inches (4cm) long, blue-grey with reddish and white stripes, devouring leaves and shoots. They spin web nests on branch forks or knit together leaves in which they hide from sprays and their natural enemy which is the cuckoo – out early in orchards to hear the munching of the first caterpillar. Once these nests were destroyed by firing a muzzle-loading gun at them with a reduced charge of powder and paper wads. Destroy the nests by hand when they are small, but spray with nicotine in early May before the caterpillars start to spin. The eggs are laid in bands round the smaller mature branches, each of which can hold as many as 200 in July and August. Cut off these branches, unless they are good, healthy spurs, or smash them with the secateurs. These eggs are immune to winter washes and so the pest is increasing.

May is the time to start pruning stone fruit such as peaches, nectarines and apricots. Go over them first for 'dieback', which is caused by a number of fungi that begin by attacking dead wood from frost or bullfinch damage, and go on to attack the living tissue, like canker in apples or pears. Snip off the dead end of any shoot and snip again and again until the wood shows clean, with no brown stain in the middle. This has the same tonic effect on the tree that extracting a decaying tooth has on a human being, and newly planted stone fruits should not be cut back to shape them at planting time like apples, but left till May in case any damage done when moving them has caused dieback.

Peaches can fruit on small spurs, but mostly on the long shoots that grew the previous year. Tie these and their older companions into the wires, if they are growing on a wall (as they usually are). When they have fruited, wait till the following May and cut them back to three or four buds – whichever points along the wall – and tie in the shoots when they are young and bendy. Another type of shoot rushes straight up, thick and strong, from the base, and this should be cut right back to the first sideways-pointing bud; this is the policy for any shoot that points awkwardly out away from the wall. If you want to cover the wall, the fruited shoots should be left alone to grow from the tips. This means fruit further and further from the centre of the fan, while hard pruning means more in the middle.

Give the first thinning at pruning time, removing one from each pair of fruitlets so they are not more than six inches (15 cm) apart all over the tree. Thinning is important because while good varieties should fruit every year, those that are raised from stones get about eight years' rest until there is a spring gentle enough to miss the blossom. Apricots flower earliest of all, and the reason many of the old walled gardens of England had walls built double, with chimneys along them, was so that rubbish could be burned between to warm the brick from inside in the days when head gardeners relied on instinct and the look of the frosty stars rather than well-dressed TV weather experts hanging warning discs on isobar-lined maps.

Plums and greengages produce their fruiting spurs on one- and two-year-old shoots, therefore if you cut them back like apples you are cutting away the crop. Newly planted trees need no pruning other than the routine dieback search in May. When they are trained on walls (greengages do very well on north- or even east-facing walls), tie the fan-trained branches to the wires with non-nylon string and pinch back any side shoots that point outwards to two or three buds – whichever points along the wall. If one of the leading shoots intrudes on a window, or a branch no longer fruits, cut it out in May, but do not keep taking out the fruited two-year-old shoots as with peaches, apricots and nectarines.

Bush and standard plums need only anti-dieback snipping, and sawing out crowded or crossing branches in May. On a Victoria plum that is growing too large for a small garden, it is safe to shorten the main leaders to twelve inches (30 cm) and the side shoots to eight (20 cm) in June, as a kind of summer pruning. Even if branches break with a heavy harvest, do not saw them out until the safe season in May and June.

Victorias are the most popular and tasty plum variety, but they have long branches that break. The best policy is to buy bush, rather than standard, trees, and make stout, wooden, inverted 'V's with a good crossing crotch at the top to fit the branches. A heavy branch is a powerful lever when it is covered with fruit, and propping it reduces the length and provides a second fulcrum, so it will not tear the main branch away.

9.

June

Available for eating	Family	Sowing	Planting
Beans, broad (longpod)	7	November	–
Beans (dried or frozen)	7	May-June	–
Beet	2	March	1–1
Cabbage (summer)	4	March	July
Carrots (early)	12	March	–
Kale	4	April	June-July
Lamb's-lettuce	13	March	–
Landcress	4	March	–
Lettuce	3	March	–
Miner's lettuce	10	March	–
Onions (spring)	8	August	–
Peas (early)	7	February	–
Potatoes (early)	11	–	April-May
Radishes	4	March-August	–
Rhubarb	9	April	February
Spinach (summer)	2	February	–
Sweetcorn (frozen)	6	April-May	–
Tomatoes (bottled)	11	–	May-June

Midsummer sowings

As the year swings to the midsummer dead centre of 21 June, there is just time to fit in the final sowings of the crops that will mature for storage in the autumn, before we change over to those that grow on the 'downhill slope' of the year. The garden should be packed with food waiting for the first release of room, and the first few of anything can be eaten immature. Pick the peas hard, start the broad beans early because there will be plently, pull carrots as small as chipolata sausages and beet like golf balls. Concentrate on what you like, but experiment to find what fits the changing demands of a family, for the waste of space no small garden can afford is that which grows a crop that nobody likes, after it has had a fair trial.

The first week in July is the very latest date for sowing beet to store, but the last in June is better, with more time to build flavour and keeping qualities. Sow the large seeds only six inches (15 cm) apart each way when they go in late, and there is still enough growing time to save them if the beet blister-fly *(Begomyia betae)* arrives and lays eggs that become legless, white maggots, producing brown blisters as they tunnel. Pick off the attacked leaves and if more than four must be taken from one plant, give a teaspoonful of dried blood as a tonic and water it in.

The last carrots have to race to reach the 1½ inches (3.5 cm) across the top they need to be sure of keeping, so sow the main-crop not later than the last week in June, which can easily miss all carrot-fly problems. Thin to three inches (8 cm) apart or, ideally, sow so thinly that you do not thin at all, and leave six inches (15 cm) between rows for this last, late sowing. Sow also the last radishes of summer as a final pair of two-inch (5 cm) apart furrows to eat in August and on into Autumn, for they will grow more slowly now the year has turned.

Windermere lettuces can still be sown for a last six-week spread of frilled and heavy heads; so can Fortune, which can go in up to mid-July. The end of June should see the last picking of rhubarb, and the bed can relax and let the fruits of summer take over while it juggles with air, water and sunlight to build up its thick, black roots for forcing next spring.

The early potatoes should be flowering well, and though this is time in theory to lift them, there will be too many marble-sized tubers for economy, so wait till the petals have dropped before taking the first, thrusting the fork in well down the sides of the ridges to avoid wasting the crop by spearing, for careless forking costs spuds.

Planting the cabbage tribe
The most urgent planting, as soon as room is available, is the

Autumn Spear sprouting broccoli, to crop from September on into November. Dig up the transplanted plants from the waiting bed (which can wait on into July), hold the leaves in a bunch and cut them across the top, an inch (3 cm) above the growing point in the middle. This seemingly savage treatment reduces the area through which the leaves transpire water and is a great help to plants moved when large through waiting for other crops to finish. Take out trowel holes eighteen inches (45 cm) apart and two feet (60 cm) between rows and fill them up with water from the can, before you dig your plants. They can then go straight in after they are sliced, have the soil firmed round them and a final top watering. Winningstadt, the August-October eating cabbage, is an equally urgent candidate for the first available space.

The June and July transplanting of cabbage-tribe vegetables must often take place late and in drought, so this system works for all of them. If plants have been lost, or sowing was missed, late cabbage can be enjoyed by sowing Red Drumhead in pairs two feet (60 cm) apart each way and thinning to the best, for this kind puts down a taproot fast and missing the shock of transplanting allows it to catch up, though the heads may be rather smaller. It is a delicious cabbage, cooked or raw, and far too good to have its vitamins destroyed by pickling vinegar.

These winter crops all follow others that had manure and have their nitrogen for a quick start from the roots of the pea tribe. If they are overfed with either chemicals or manure they will grow soft and sappy, and fail to last the winter. This is particularly important with sprouting broccoli and the kales. As the peas finish, take out the sticks or stakes and wire, clip the haulm for compost, hoe off the surface weeds and trowel in the cabbage types, which all appreciate firm soil. The Sutton broad beans from the first sowing usually finish fast enough to fit in lettuce and radish where they came out, while the daffa beans for drying in August will release further room.

Celery-planting time

Winter celery is also clamouring for room, and there is no need to dig the slit-trench-size pits of the past. Dig in compost or manure if you have any to spare, or 4 oz a square yard (110 g a square metre) of blood, fish and bone if not. Then take out two wide 'V's with the hoe corner four-five inches (10-12 cm) across and three (8 cm) deep, two feet (60 cm) apart, and put in the plants at foot (30 cm) intervals along the bottom. Water them as a start and then give weekly waterings of comfrey liquid manure, which should now be ready from the mid-May cut.

By mid-August, the plants should be over a foot (30cm) high, ready for any side shoots to be broken off from their bases before the modern version of 'earthing up'. The first step needs two people – one to hold the stems bunched together and the other to slip a rubber band over the top, like those used round cos lettuces such as Little Gem or Winter Density to bring them on to delicious long crispness in about four days.

Then heap soil shovelled from between the rows to fill the furrows and go about three inches (8cm) up the stems – again easier with two people, one each side of the row. Three weeks later, heap leaf-mould or peat from both sides of the row right up to the bunched leaves at the top of the sticks to ensure freedom from frost. Whack the sides flat and firm with the spade and protect the covering from washing down with fifteen-inch (38cm) squares of flat asbestos, or even glass – anything that will last without rotting in the rain and store flat in the shed for use year after year. Take off the squares, spread the leaf-mould and dig the celery as required.

The best leaf-mould for this will be the mowings-hastened heap made from last autumn's leaves, which should be ready by early September. Peat is expensive, but this is a good end for a bale that has been bought and used to store root vegetables in for three years and that may now hold storage-rot spores. Celery is not a rotated crop, so it can fit wherever the right space is ready at the right time, and the ground levelled ready for the next crop which will appreciate the humus.

Organic pest and weed control in June

There will be plenty of mowings available in June and July, with ample comfrey as the bed matures. If there is a comfrey surplus beyond the need for liquid-manure production, especially when the first blossoms on the first tomato trusses are showing pea-sized fruitlets, spread some between the tomato rows and between the bush fruit. Covered down with mowings and kept well away from the stems, this will suppress weeds and make surface compost. If the garden is troubled with a wasp nest of the type that shows as a tunnel (like a mousehole) in a bank, with such steady traffic in and out that one almost expects to see an enterprising beetle outside selling evening papers, wait till well after sunset and dump a barrowload of mowings on top.

This will heat and demand oxygen, which it can take from the supply inside the wasp nest and by morning it will have killed the lot without poison or problems.

Weeds grow fast in June, and where perennials such as creeping buttercup between bush fruit are hard to dig and not easy to kill with a mowings mulch, newspapers are an answer. Save or get from neighbours any large newspaper printed on good-quality paper, for four thicknesses of each, weighed down with stones, will exclude light most effectively from June onwards. For paths, try a mixture of creosote in boiling water, in a proportion of 1–8, sprinkled on the weeds in dry weather when there will be minimum run-off. Do not get it on your skin, or on the lawn or plants. It contains phenols which have a soil bacterium to break them down and as creosote is a product of wood distillation, it will not leave anything permanent in the path, where nothing eats. It is cheaper and more effective than a blowlamp or a flame gun, which takes a long time merely to kill off surface weeds.

The key to weedkilling by organic methods is timing. Cutting docks in the first week in June, so that they make safe compost material before the seeds ripen, and again in September, does the maximum damage to monster specimens. This also kills out ragwort. For thistles, remember the saying, 'Cut in June and cut too soon, cut in July 'tis sure to die' from the many small farmers who cleared their fields by careful cutting and the modern organic farmers who time their silage cuts to control their weeds without spreading dock seeds in the manure from the cattle that eat the silage. If large quantities of mowings can be obtained from a sports ground in June, this is the best time to pile them at least a foot (30cm) deep on really bad perennial weeds such as ground elder and convolvulus. The idea is to have them thick enough to heat and mat to a solid, slimy mess which will exclude light and air at a season when the weeds need these most in their maximum growth period.

The root secretions of *Tagetes minuta,* a relative of French and African marigolds, will kill ground elder, and convolvulus less effectively, if planted a foot (30cm) apart each way into weeds that have merely been cut down, though most people plant after they have cleared the bed, to kill the left-in roots. Sow in March on a window-sill or in April in the open, and pot or transplant when the seedlings are about a foot (30cm) high in June. They will grow to ten feet (3m) by October or November, producing a mass of compost material with a strong, antiseptic smell used to repel fleas in Africa, where it has run wild.

The stems can be as thick as a thumb and need bashing with an axe-back on something hard so they break down. The ground-elder roots will be found blackened and hollow from the effect of the thiophenes in the root secretions used by some plants as weapons in the underground wars they fight. However, this cannot be used to clear out ground elder and convolvulus from a border, for the roots of the weeds can hide in the herbaceous-plant clumps. The small star-like flowers of *T. minuta* in October arrive too late to set any seed in this country, so there is no risk of it becoming a worse weed than the ones it kills (as it is in Australia, where it is called 'Stinking Rogers' after the amateur gardener who let it escape).

Organic fruit care in June

June is pruning time for cherries when, in addition to the search and snip for dieback as for all stone fruit, three to four inches (8-10cm) of each strong, young shoot can be removed, to put more strength into ripening blossom buds along the rest of the shoot for the next year and to take out the soft growth which the cherry blackfly *(Myzus cerasi)* attacks first, on the principle of pinching out the tips of broad beans to stop their blackfly. This is not very effective, because cherry shoots stay young for so much of their length and the small side shoots, which should be pinched back to two or three buds – whichever points along the wall – are equally attractive to the aphids.

One way round is to paint a grease band on the trunk, taking care to paint the wall behind it too, and a strip along the house wall to stop ants carrying up blackfly as 'house cows'. This is far more effective for bush or standard cherries which need only a dieback search and the removal of worn-out, crowding or crossing branches.

The other trick is to persuade your neighbours to hang fat for the tits in their ornamental cherries, so the eggs will be eaten and there will be fewer blackfly to migrate and attack your trees. A cane can be thrust in so the fat hangs about three feet (1 m) from the wall to keep it out of starling range, but the tits cannot get between the branches and the bricks. Nicotine can be used in aphid strength in June, which spares the twenty-two-spot ladybird *(Thea 22-Punctata)*. Cherry blackfly repels the ordinary seven-spot species, but the twenty-two spotter which

JUNE 119

is cream with black spots and looks like a tiny chessboard, eats them so greedily that it builds up a population that can keep the pest within limits.

Apart from birds, defeated by nylon netting hung in front of the wall, the main loss of fruit, applying also to peaches, nectarines and apricots, is 'June drop' which is a natural thinning from trees in the open, but increased for wall specimens because narrow beds beside houses are often very dry. Run a hose in the bed at least once a week through June to give a real soaking, but when planting any fruit against a house wall, make sure that the soil is not heaped above the damp course in a raised bed, for repeated soakings will suck into the brickwork and mean damp stains and peeling wallpaper for the room inside. Wall fruits have relatively weak roots so do no harm by drawing water from under the foundations, but never plant a poplar weeping willow or anything fast-growing closer than twenty feet (6m) from a house.

In June it is possible to catch codling-moth caterpillars before they burrow into the fruit, but a policy of grease banding is the best *preventative*. The inorganic can waste a considerable sum and do a great deal of hard work spraying for the pests and diseases they *might* have, when these can be rare, or controlled already by milder methods. If last year's apples had maggots in, then it is worth spraying in mid-June with nicotine to spare ladybirds and catch the small caterpillars – no later than ten days after the fall of the blossom petals. Keep a lookout in June and July for any fruitlets with holes in the sides, or any that drop, for these should be destroyed with the grubs inside.

The pea moth *(Cydia nigricans)* lays its eggs between early June and the end of August and once inside the pod the caterpillars are safe from spraying, becoming the familiar maggots found when shelling peas and a real problem for those who grow peas for drying. Spray with nicotine soap or derris about a week after the first flowering and again a fortnight later, to catch the caterpillars when they are crawling outside, like codling-moth caterpillars on the fruitlets.

Cutworms or surface caterpillars are active and can slaughter newly planted cabbage plants, so bring out the painted tins and stand them over the seedlings, and also over lettuce. There is a gain anyway from the effect of shelter and warmth from the sun on the black surface. Tins will also baffle slugs which will not climb vertically up a tall tin, but as this trick shades the plant if left on for a whole wet summer, it is only useful for protecting treasures for short periods.

There are many trapping methods, including putting out soup plates full of equal parts of milk and water, and clearing out the drowned slugs with a broom and refuelling; while beer, sweetened with brown sugar is a good but expensive filling for the 'slug pub', a plastic gadget that is proof against cats, hedgehogs and rain. A cheaper remedy is the old Belgian and French one of sinking a wine bottle with the neck level with the soil surface, and just half an inch or so of beer at the bottom. The slugs crawl in attracted by the scent and cannot climb out of the smooth sides. When beer traps for slugs were invented, landlords would present the contents of the drip trays free to good-customer gardeners but today, in an ecology-minded age, they 'recycle' the froth spilled from drawing pints, and the slugs get nothing on the house.

Collecting slugs by the thousand on warm June nights (with 10-11 pm the best hunting period) is tedious, and slicing them through with a tin blade hammered sharp on the end of a broomstick is not for the squeamish, though the bodies attract other slugs so more can be massacred. Metaldehyde and other poisons also kill the hedgehogs which are the best natural controllers, and can also poison cats and dogs. Two safe substances are Fertosan slug destroyer, based on aluminium sulphate (a harmless substance also used by alpine gardeners to cancel out lime by its lock-up effect for lime-hating gentians), and a mixture of one part of alum and seven parts of slaked lime. Mix the two very thoroughly and scatter thinly on the surface on mild moist evenings.

Biological control for cabbage caterpillars

There is now a biological control for the cabbage-white, diamond-back and tomato-moth caterpillars, which hits only these, and is useless against gooseberry sawfly and the swarming pests of fruit. It will not, therefore, run wild and clear all the moths and butterflies of Britain. This is Thuricide, a culture of spores of *Bacillus thuringiensis*, to be made up in water and sprayed when the first caterpillars are seen feeding. One treatment lasts a season.

Many repellent methods are suggested. Spraying the cabbage crop with a half-and-half solution of milk and water when the cabbage whites are seen fluttering purposefully over the bed, at approximately weekly intervals, has worked for many people who, however, rarely report their failures.

When June is dry and there is not enough rain to beat down the winged stage of the mealy-cabbage aphid *(Brevicoryne brassicae)*, this creature can swarm, spreading from farm crops to gardens, and producing 'plagues' of ladybirds. On a normal diet of broad-bean blackfly and greenfly off roses, a female ladybird will lay about 120 eggs a season, each hatching to a aphid-eating larva; but on mealy-cabbage aphid the egg rate shoots up to 600-800. Moreover, the females do not count the calories when they find this nutritious food, but eat until the autumn sees millions of WX and outsize ladybirds with a far better chance of coming safely through the next winter. They do their best to keep up with the aphid epidemics which are increased by heavy chemical nitrogen dressings producing extra nutritious sap and more readily attacked crops in farms and gardens. Help them by spraying with nicotine to spare them to carry on their good work.

From the end of May to mid-July the gooseberry aphis *(Aphis grossularia)* spends a summer holiday sucking the tips of gooseberry shoots, and sometimes those of red- and black-currants, twisting the leaves so badly that it is impossible to kill it by spraying. It then returns to the guelder-rose, the wild viburnum of the hedges. Very many hedges have been destroyed by farmers, but our gardens contain many species of viburnum which provide winter homes for this quite serious pest. If it arrives, snip about three inches (8cm) off the tips of the gooseberry shoots and burn these or dump them in the dustbin. This also acts as a kind of summer pruning which improves the fruit buds for next season, and means fewer aphids which are not doing your viburnums any good either.

10.

July

Available for eating	Family	Sowing	Planting
Beans, broad (longpod)	7	November	–
Beans (dried or frozen)	7	May-June	–
Beans, French	7	May	–
Beet (fresh)	2	March	–
Cabbage	4	June	July
Carrots (early)	12	March	–
Cauliflowers	4	February	April
Celery	12	March-April	May-June
Kale	4	April	June-July
Kohl rabi	4	March-April	–
Lamb's-lettuce	13	May	–
Landcress	4	May	–
Lettuce	3	April	–
Miner's lettuce	10	May	–
Onions (spring)	8	March	–
Peas (early)	7	February	–
Potatoes (early)	11	–	April-May
Radishes	4	March-August	–
Spinach, New Zealand	1	March	–
Spinach (summer)	2	April	–
Tomatoes (bottled)	11	–	May-June

July sees the early potatoes lifted row by row, with their haulm taken to the compost heap. Before planting anything after potatoes, dig over the bed to remove any left-in tubers, which will not only be weeds growing in the wrong place next year, but also carry the spores of potato blight, *Phytophthora infestans.*

Potato-blight problem
This shows first in cold, dull, moist weather in July as rounded dark-brown patches round the edges of the leaves which spread rapidly and blacken the whole haulm, including the stems. This reduces the food supply to the tubers so there is a tiny crop, and the spores wash down from the foliage through the soil, infecting the potatoes and causing them to rot when stored. The best preventive measure is to choose blight-resisting varieties such as Maris Peer or Wilja (second earlies), or Croft, Desiree, Kerr's Pink or Stormont Enterprise among maincrops, but none are nearly 100 per cent blight-proof. Therefore, when the moist dark-brown patches show first at the tips of the leaves, spray with Burgundy mixture or Bordeaux mixture which can be bought ready for mixing.

If the disease continues to spread, cut down all the haulm and take it away for composting, for blight does not live long on the foliage and is killed at 120°F (50°C). Wait for three weeks before lifting the potatoes to give any spores on the surface time to die out. At intervals, pick over the small crop that remains, for blighted tubers rot and this spreads to others in contact with them.

In dull, cold summers, spray first in the last week in June, spray again three weeks later, and a third time in another three weeks, using Burgundy mixture because it has some spore-killing effect. In the Midlands spray first in mid-July and in the north towards the end of the month. This preventive spray will keep the blight off and it is routine for commercial growers – organic and inorganic. Most gardeners trust to luck, immune varieties and the fact that garden plots are so scattered that the disease misses many of them, though it sweeps through allotments.

The disease is far worse in tomatoes, which share membership of the order *Solanaceae* with potatoes (which catch it first). Unless July is dry and bright, spray with Burgundy mixture during the first week in July in the south and early August in the north, and spray every two weeks. The spores blow from potato crops and go quite high in moist weather, so they can arrive from a distance. The disease shows as large, russet-brown, marbled areas on the green fruit and dark brown streaks on leaves and stems. There are no immune tomato varieties and if there is potato blight in your district, spray. Keep a tin of Burgundy or Bordeaux mixture in stock.

The tomatoes will need their side shoots removing, and tying as they grow taller, tying a first knot firmly round the stake, and then one beyond the stem where the loop can get a grip under a leaf. Tomato plants often fork about a foot (30cm) from the ground and both shoots can be trained up the stake, but not more. Outdoor tomatoes can yield 8lb (4kg) of fruit each, and with a variety that ripens well off the plants – like Harbinger, for bottling and deep freezing – they are a storing crop like apples, rather than a few weeks of eating and then too much green fruit for chutney.

Give them a weekly feed with liquid comfrey, and there is no reason why this, or seaweed foliar feed, should not be added to Bordeaux or Burgundy mixtures, for there is no chemical reaction between them. Syringing the leaves with seaweed feed can increase the crop, but only where the soil is short of a mineral, for plants (like trees) never take through their leaves what they can gather through their roots.

Chinese radish and cabbage take-away

Midsummer Day was high noon and it is already late enough to sow the Chinese radishes and cabbages which bolt swiftly to seed if sown in the morning of the year. There are three varieties of these radishes, all excellent winter vegetables to grate raw in salads from October even to April, or to cook like turnips with a radish flavour. China Rose is the best known, red and white, like a giant French Breakfast, but up to four inches (10cm) in diameter and six or even eight (15-20cm) long, growing up to 1½lb (750g) of root from a foot (30cm) of row. Sow it in July or August in inch-deep (2.5cm) furrows eight inches (20cm) apart, with the large seeds in pairs at six-inch (15cm) intervals, thinned to the best of each. They can be lifted and stored like carrots in October or left in to dig as required.

Black Spanish is also known as 'Bavarian' because it is served raw and sliced into sticks in beer halls, where its stronger flavour is reputed to encourage beer drinking among the rare Bavarians who need encouragement. This is grown in exactly the same way, but it has a black skin so needs peeling rather than just scrubbing and is turnip- rather than radish-shaped. As this kind sits on the surface and can get eaten by slugs it is best dug and stored.

Japanese All Seasons is long and pale cream, rather like a white Icicle radish but up to a foot (30cm) long and two inches (5cm) across the top. This does well on sandy soils for its long, tapered root will go down over eighteen inches (45cm) after moisture. Unlike the other two, it can also be sown in March or April for summer eating, scrubbed and sliced for salads or fried as 'radish chips'. It is best left in to dig as needed, because it will not keep if the long taproot is broken.

The Chinese cabbage is *Brassica pekinensis*, an entirely different species from the ancestors of our cabbage tribe, but it still gets clubroot, so should be grown in the cabbage section of the rotation. The best variety is Pei Tsai, which looks like a pale-green cos lettuce, about fifteen inches (38cm) high. Greengrocers are now selling it as 'Chinese leaves' for salads. From July sowings it will be ready from September on into autumn, finishing in the hard frosts of November.

Sow the large seeds like the radishes, but eight inches (20cm) apart in the rows. Neither the cabbages nor the radishes cross with our familiar varieties and seed is easily saved by sowing when the day length is *increasing*, letting the pods ripen and split before putting them in chitting trays to dry.

Chinese cabbage has always been handicapped by sowing at the wrong season and cooking the wrong way. Unlike our cabbage tribe, the Chinese species contains no sulphur, so produces no smell when cooking, and those who are allergic to the cabbage race should try if they can eat it safely. There is a new variety, Sanpan, which can be sown in April to enjoy in summer, but this is an F_1 hybrid, so seed cannot be saved. A modernized Chinese recipe is to slice the cabbage lengthways and then crossways, after removing the outer leaves. Heat some soya or corn oil in a frying pan and drop in a quarter cabbage which will exude enough juice to make water unnecessary, and then drop in the rest. Simmer in its own juice for about eight minutes and serve with the distinctive flavour that made it 'sell like hot cabbages' in China to the tea-clipper Captains who brought them to England in the 1840s.

Swedes and turnips are better sown now for winter storage, after an earlier sowing at the end of March for those who like them from May onwards. They are tastier grown fast to tennis-ball size than the heavy cannon balls greengrocers crash into the scales. Sow in half-inch (1 cm) deep furrows eight inches (20cm) apart and thin to eight (20cm) between plants. Those who like turnip leaves as a green vegetable can pick from their plants after these have been sown four weeks (without robbing the same specimens each time), as though they were winter spinach, and still enjoy their roots without loss of quality, but losing some yield.

Leeks and onions

Gardeners today rarely have room to grow the leeks like bolsters that won prizes at forgotten flower shows. July planting after early potatoes brings two-inch (5cm) thick stems, while if they wait till August they will be only as fat as candles, but just as good if you only have room to spare then. Make holes eight inches (20cm) apart along a garden line, with a long dibber (use an old spade or fork handle with the end repointed; or an edging tool with the blade broken off, which gives nice steel-shod tip). Drop a leek plant, roots first, down each hole, fill this with water, move the line eight inches (20cm) and plant another row. Teach your family to enjoy leeks, for these have no clubroot and are perhaps our easiest winter vegetable.

Onions from sets, and the Japanese autumn-sown variety Express Yellow, will be ready well ahead of the spring-sown varieties, and their leaf tips yellow in July, ready to be bent over at rather more than a right angle to the ground so the necks break and they begin to ripen. Leave them ten days to dry, and dig them up to lie in the ever-useful potato-chitting trays; stack these one on top of each other in a shed at night or during wet weather and put out in the sun. These fast onions not only leave room earlier for a wider choice of crops to follow them, but give a better chance of getting good weather for drying the bulbs thoroughly.

Wring off the onion tops for burning or dustbin dumping because of the risk of a late compost heap failing to heat sufficiently to kill fungus spores, and drop the bulbs down the legs of laddered tights – the more ladders the better because this improves the ventilation through the nylon. Open-weave or 'fishnet' stockings were best, but these are no longer readily available, and tights offer a pair of onion-storing containers to hang by their middles in a dry attic. Attics can get very hot in the warm days of spring and it is worth re-sorting the onions into greengrocer's nets as used for pumpkins, removing any that have gone soft, and hanging them in a cooler place, for after April the problem is to stop them sprouting.

Organic pest control in July

Look along your lettuce rows for any plants flopping suddenly. Dig these up and you will find yellow or grey aphids eating the roots. These are the lettuce-root aphis *(Pemphigus bursarius)* which spend most of the year on poplar trees, but spend summer holidays on sow-thistle and lettuce roots. Water the rows with cigarette-end nicotine, allowing seventy-two hours before eating the lettuces. Though some organic gardeners 'make friends with their weeds', there is the problem of the friends of your friends, and lettuce-root aphid also associate with fat-hen and good king henry, its perennial relative.

During this month most of the cabbage-tribe plants will be out and growing and the cabbage-white fly will be arriving to lay its tiny eggs that will become the swarms that rise in clouds from our cabbages. Composting this pest, as given in Chapter 3, is one answer, but not to the extra arrivals from other gardens. Work at Beltsville (the US equivalent to Rothamstead) has shown that lengths of hardboard as used for weevil trapping, coated first with a bright yellow paint (the best shade is 'Gold Cup' gloss) and when dry with a light motor oil which stays both sticky and transparent, trap the closely related white fly of tomatoes most effectively.

This is not a pest of outdoor tomatoes and the 100 per cent success of the idea of planting French marigolds between the rows is explained by the fact that the tomato fly stays in the greenhouse, while the cabbage species, which looks exactly the same, sticks to cabbages. The tiny wasp, *Encarsia formosa*, is the effective biological control for tomato white fly, but cannot be relied upon to make a timely appearance, so the board trick is well worth using. The oil companies do not yet advertise any special grade for this make of pest, so buy the cheapest. This should work just as well for the cabbage-white fly.

Summer pruning and pest control

Hard pruning in winter makes apples and pears grow more wood, because the roots have less growth to support, which is why sawing branches out of an elderly tree (especially if some are cankered) can give it new vigour. Summer pruning in July 'slims' trees growing too big for small gardens by reducing the carbohydrate intake from the sunlight on the living leaves, and so cutting down their calories.

Shorten the leaders by a quarter of their length and the side shoots by two thirds. The prunings are soft in July and can go straight on the compost heap. The effect is to put more strength into ripening fruit buds rather than growing more wood. It has also put your tree 'on a diet' and reduced its growth speed, which is important if it was grafted on an ordinary crab-apple stock and not one of the new dwarfing varieties.

At winter pruning time reduce the leaders so they are left with a third of their first length, and their lesser contemporaries to three or four buds – whichever points away from the centre of the tree. This is exactly the pruning recommended for February – the difference is that you have gone over the tree quickly in summer first to have fewer leaves working, and gained better ripening of fruiting buds.

In late July, the summer pruning of cordon apples and pears consists of snipping back any new, young shoots from the main stem to three leaves and any from the existing shoots to a single leaf. Horizontally trained trees should have their side shoots shortened to three leaves each. Both types of trained tree are pruned hard because, like wall peaches, cherries and plums, they are grown intensively in little space.

The June drop is now over and it is time for the final thinning of peaches, nectarines and apricots. When the fruitlets are the size of thumbnails, thin to eight inches (20cm) between them. This is approximate, for if you have a strong branch with only about seven fruit on it, all crowded up one end, leave them all on even if they are only four inches (10cm) apart, which just stops them touching each other. It also pays to thin Kirke's Blue, the rare flavour plum that does well on walls.

The best control for codling moth in apples is to tie bands of sacking round the base of the trunks. 'Mutton cloth', which is cotton cloth of similar texture that covers mutton carcasses when delivered frozen to the butcher (the meat equivalent to polythene bags for the deepfreeze), is a modern substitute for sacking. Put these bands on during the first week in July and take them off in October. The full-fed caterpillars drop to the ground or fall in the fruit after four weeks' feeding, and many of them will try to climb the trees again to hibernate in the bark crevices. The sacking or mutton cloth folded into four or five thicknesses about eight inches (20cm) across, tied at the top with string and a few inches above ground level, below the grease-band paint, will give them an apparently ideal hibernation place. It can be cut off and burned in October, or given to the chickens. Ducks or chickens in an orchard clear a great many of these caterpillars.

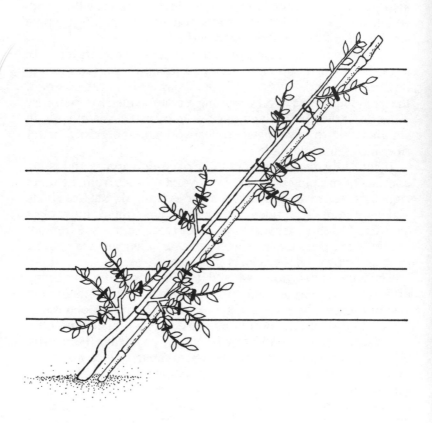

8 Cordon – at summer pruning

Collect fallen apples at least once a week so that the sawfly larvae, which pupate in the ground, do not get a chance to finish off and escape. If any apple appears to be ripening ahead of the others, pick it, for it probably has a sawfly larvae or two in it, and if you cut it up you will have saved more apples than if you had left it on. Too many windfall apples are bad for poultry, but pigs enjoy them and so do horses and cattle. Windfall apples bottle well for cooking and with bruises and livestock discarded, keep perfectly. Those who have windfalls often give them away, so apples for the winter can be enjoyed just for the cost of heating fuel and jars by those who do not even have gardens.

Do not forget a final sowing of Little Gem, Fortune or any other fast lettuce to last on into autumn, slowed by the shortening days. The aim of organic gardening is to grow better and more healthy food in every sense from every garden, and this should include salads right round the year.

11.

August

Available for eating	Family	Sowing	Planting
Beans, broad (Windsor)	7	May	–
Beans, French	7	May	–
Beans, runner	7	–	May
Beet (fresh)	2	March	–
Cabbage	4	June	July
Carrots (early)	12	March	–
Carrots (Shorthorn)	12	March	–
Cauliflowers	4	February	April
Celery	12	March-April	May-June
Cucumbers (outdoors)	5	April	–
Kale	4	April	June-July
Kohl rabi	4	April-May	–
Lamb's-lettuce	13	May	–
Landcress	4	May	–
Lettuce	3	April	–
Marrows; Courgettes	5	April	–
Miner's lettuce	10	May	–
Onions	8	March	–
Onions (spring)	8	March	–
Peas (maincrop)	7	April	–
Potatoes (early)	11	–	March
Radishes	4	March-August	–
Spinach, New Zealand	1	March	–
Spinach (summer)	2	April	–
Sweetcorn	6	April-May	1–1
Tomatoes (outdoor)	11	–	May

August sowings for winter and spring

There are still weeks of growing weather left and time to sow the winter and spring leaf crops in two stages – one now and one in September. Lifting the onions early, with even the sown crop finished by the end of the month, releases more ground, and there is space between the wide-spaced cabbage tribe for sowing landcress, lamb's-lettuce and miner's lettuce. The August sowings, which will be eaten before the later crops like broccoli, kale and January King cabbages, can well go between them without the risk of being trampled in the snow or when driving in stakes. Sprouting broccoli, kale and Brussels sprouts are tall and have a considerable sail area in autumn gales, so short, strong stakes to reach about a foot (30cm) out of the ground, driven in on the side of the stems away from the prevailing wind and tied firmly with good string, will save root breakages.

Autumn-sown onions do not need firm soil because by the time they want something to push against, the ground will have firmed in ten months without digging. Organic fertilizers or even compost should not be dug in either, for winter crops can suffer in hard winters if they have too much nitrogen. They will do very well on what they gather from the autumn and late-summer peak of bacterial activity that is usually snatched by chickweed. Compost and rotted manure dug under in autumn is for ground that is to be sown with green manure crops in September or October.

White Lisbon onions can be sown as August ends or September begins, in half-inch (1 cm) deep furrows eight inches (20cm) apart on ground raked level and smooth, aiming at an inch (2.5cm) between seeds. Those who are really fond of spring onions can sow single or even half rows in early March, in April and May.

Solidity, the British onion for autumn sowing, and Express Yellow, the Japanese, can both be sown in the same way, but thinned to six inches (15cm) apart, and the thinnings eaten as 'spring onions'. There is a risk in growing them too large from earlier sowings so they run to seed, but in Scotland and the north, early August is not too soon if they are to be growing well before winter. They will be helped by feeding with comfrey liquid manure in March and April.

Winter lettuces can be sown from early August in rows a foot (30cm) apart and thinned to this much between them as

September ends, because if they do not touch each other they are safer from slugs. Winter Density, the hardiest cos, can go closer and so can the old Arctic King, about eight inches (20cm) each way, but Imperial Winter or Valdor, larger and newer kinds, need the wider spacing. The thinnings can be transplanted onto a sunny bed, between tomatoes, if the final pickings can be made carefully, and the plants taken up without treading on the lettuce crop, to heart up in spring. Hoe off the weeds and take them away, for slugs are designed to clean up decaying vegetable wastes – and lettuces too, so the less food left for them on the surface in winter the better. September sowings are late to transplant, but these two can be made between tomato rows, with the protection of wire pea-guards – not against birds, but careless feet.

Lettuce is non-rotational and can fit anywhere that has time to let the spring-hearting crop finish, and it fits well on the sunny bed on a south-facing slope that rotates tomatoes, drying beans, and pumpkins and cucumbers. The spinach tribe is also non-rotational, and can follow lettuce or drying beans, sown in August or September between the rows after merely hoeing, although caution is needed at harvest and clearing. Nothing can be sown between pumpkins or cucumbers, so the border can rest after digging, composting and manuring.

Sow broad-leafed prickly spinach (it has prickly *seeds*, not leaves – unlike the round-seeded summer varieties) in clusters eight inches (20cm) apart, and fifteen (38cm) between rows, to allow room to walk between them for picking. Perpetual spinach sown in the same way has rather lower oxalic acid and stands longer into the spring, but Swiss or Ruby chard is by far the most rewarding of this group of winter crops. Spare it eighteeen inches (45cm) between the rows to allow the big leaves to be twisted off more easily. Sow sufficient of them that there is no need to pick any too hard, and give them time to grow and stand the winter, always where the previous crop had the manure.

August fruit harvest

August is traditionally a month for holidays, but leaving a garden full of food should make it easier to find a neighbour to water, trim tomato plants, and pick fruit, in return for a share of the produce. The September routine will be much the same, and a policy of, 'You look after my garden and I look after yours,' could well be arranged between organic-gardening neighbours.

Make aprons to hold Kilner jars and pick direct into these, so that soft fruit can be tipped into plastic containers and put in the deep freeze within an hour of leaving the bushes, or bottled within three. As soon as soft fruit is picked, it starts to lose Vitamin C – especially blackcurrants, which are the best source. Vitamin C is also destroyed by light, and in health-conscious Sweden they use brown glass milk bottles to reduce the losses. Therefore, keep your bottled fruit in a dark cupboard or stacked in closed cartons in the attic. It has been found that cutting the three-to-four day gap between field and kitchen via market, wholesaler and greengrocer to a few hours, and storage in darkness showed twice as much Vitamin C in blackcurrants bottled six months earlier, than in a sample bought 'fresh' in London. Vitamin C varies according to the variety and Table 15 shows the average content, picked over a seven-year period at Long Ashton Research Station in a trial with fruit taken direct to the laboratory to give accurate analysis.

Table 15: Average Vitamin C content of blackcurrants according to variety

	Vitamin C Mg per 100g
Baldwin	242
Seabrook's Black	205
Wellington's XXX	204
Davidson's Eight	203
Westwick Choice	235
Boskoop Giant	198
Mendip Cross	196

The fruit really worth making jam with are strawberries, for these neither freeze nor bottle well, and their delicious flavour justifies the quantity of white sugar that jam making adds to our diets. Blackcurrants and raspberries are better value bottled without any sugar at all. All fruit is designed to be eaten at peak ripeness when its vitamins and flavour are at their best, and their seeds in ideal condition for natural sowing. When we eat carrots we are (from the viewpoint of the carrot) stealing the hoarded food that should have thrust up a tall seed head to toss its personal harvest high and wide upon the wind. Fruit 'wants' to be eaten, providing colour contrast to draw the flying customers and taste to build up the 'brand loyalty' that will bring the same customers year after year to spread the seeds in their bodies as effectively as blackberries, briars and hawthorns are sown on almost every ungrazed acre.

As the cost of even pick-it-yourself soft fruit soars like the price of the petrol to reach it, soft fruit becomes a better and better bargain in every garden. The cheapest counter-measure against the birds, which are the bushes' favourite customers, is a temporary fruit cage. Make tripods with six-foot (2m) bamboo canes tied firmly about two inches (5cm) from the top with a 'wigwam' effect and cap each with a jam-jar. These serve to support nylon netting draped generously over them sliding on their smoothness without tearing and leave room to get inside for picking. A metal fruit cage with doors is of course better, but with care to redrape the net side after every picking, the bamboo and jar system saves money and can be stored bundled and labelled until next summer. (It is important to know which net fits where when they are wanted again.)

A valuable written guide is *Home Preservation of Fruit and Vegetables* (Ministry of Agriculture, Fisheries and Food Bulletin No. 21, HMSO), which can be bought direct or ordered through a bookshop. It offers the most concise and practical help on the subject, and compares very favourably with expensive books that are rich in pictures and padding, but poor on solutions to preservation problems.

The test for ripeness in sweetcorn is to feel if the cobs are plump and firm and the silky tassel beyond the green sheath is withering and turning brown. Then turn back the sheath, remove a grain and press it with a thumbnail – the juice should come out rather like Devonshire cream. Do *not* wait till the grains are hard, or you will have wasted time and space on growing expensive chicken food. After a few tries the state of the tassel tells the ripeness and readiness for freezing as well as eating freely from now until the frosts.

Tomatoes too will be ripening and it pays to pick at the light-red stage rather than wait until they are rich red and the birds attack. Blackbirds are especially fond of tomatoes and though a bamboo-tripod fruit cage can give complete protection, this makes spraying, trimming, tying and watering awkward, so pick less ripe to keep the birds waiting for real-red ripeness, while your fruit finishes safely indoors.

Cut out the canes

As each raspberry variety finishes, cut out the canes that have fruited, remembering that some, like Malling Exploit, will bear an autumn crop as well. This gets rid of the raspberry aphis *(Amphorophora idaci)* and lets the sun in to ripen the young canes which grow ahead ready for their autumn pruning. Burn the canes because they can hold spores of raspberry rust and cane blight as well as aphid eggs.

Raspberries often show virus symptoms, with the leaves turning yellow and their veins staying green, but because cutting out the fruited canes removes a larger proportion of wood than from any other pruning operation every year, an established bed can lose a great many minerals, especially magnesium. Try a seaweed spray on the leaves and 8 oz a square yard (220g a square metre) of ground dolomite at pruning time, before grubbing out the bed. If it is still fruiting well, water an ounce (28g) of Epsom salts in a two gallon (9 litre) can along twelve feet (4m) of row the following May as a quicker remedy. There is a virus, carried by the aphid, but it is not common.

Boysenberries (a cross between a blackberry and a loganberry, larger and tastier than either) of which the thornless variety is a pleasure to prune, and the loganberries, of which the thornless variety is less sharp in taste, should also have their fruited canes cut out to leave room for the young shoots that will fruit the following year to be tied in loosely to wait for pruning in October. Blackberries fruit later, on both the old and young wood, so should wait till December.

Pest control by pruning

In August look for American gooseberry mildew *(Sphaerotheca mors-uvae)*, which is a white fungus on leaves, stems and berries that later turns brown. Cut off the shoot tips in August with about four inches (10cm) of stem, because this is where the spores that spread the disease concentrate. Then spray the bushes with ½ lb (220g) of soft soap (the genuine article, made with potassium carbonate, not caustic soda) and 1 lb (450g) of ordinary washing soda, in five gallons (22 litres) of cold water. Spray again in the spring when they start to flower and again when the fruit is well set. This fungicide, which is weaker than lime-sulphur, spares Anthocoris, does not harm varieties that are 'sulphur shy' (few gardeners know their older gooseberries by name), and serves also for the less-common European gooseberry mildew *(Microsphaera grossulariae)*. This is thin and scanty, stays white and is mainly on the leaves, unlike the American species which is chiefly on stems and berries. Try the 1–3 strength urine on this one, because it is a powdery mildew on the surface.

Red and white currants, unlike black, fruit on the old wood as apples do, and can therefore be trained as cordons or fans against house or shed walls, growing in narrow beds where they can be easily protected from birds by a hanging nylon curtain. Summer prune these by pinching out the tips of new side shoots in August to strengthen the fruiting buds round their bases. After the leaves fall, shorten these shoots to an inch (2.5 cm), and new growth on leaders – reaching up the wall or across it – by a third of their length.

Blackcurrants are pruned in November, but look over the bushes in August (also red and white currants when summer pruning) for shoots with withered leaves or leaves and fruit dwarfed. Cut these out for burning, snipping again if there is a tunnel inside, and go on snipping till the wood is clean and white. This is caused by the creamy-white caterpillar, with black spots and a brown head, of the currant clearwing moth *(Aegeria tipuliformis)*, eating away safe from spraying inside the branches, which can be a serious problem if it gets established in a garden.

Start strawberry beds in August

August is the best month for starting a strawberry bed, for if they go in now or in September there is a good chance of a crop next year. Organic gardeners rotate their strawberry beds like other crops, partly as a disease-control measure and partly to use the humus from the bed through the vegetable garden. The principle is to plant each year at the end of one of the rotation beds, and start another each year, using either bought plants or runners from your own bed, so that there are four – one at each stage, from freshly planted to four years old, and with a falling yield. Dig the oldest one up, and replant at the other end of the same bed, then dig over the old site ready to go under vegetables.

This method has the disadvantage of having four small strawberry beds instead of a single large one, but it is rather

easier to surround four beds with low wirenetting on short
stakes that can be moved to second ends in turn, and cover each
with a net that is small enough to roll up for picking, weeding or
spraying, than to bend double under a large, low construction.
Alternatively, have five beds, each in turn under four years'
strawberries, though this means clearing a whole bed in August
or September and a dip in yield. Six plots would be better: a
good long rotation and a spare bed for extra crops.

Start each strawberry square with a good barrow-load of
compost or well-rotted manure to four square yards or metres,
and 3 lb (1.3 kg) of fine bonemeal, dug in with the manure tucked
well down in the trenches. Strawberries are phosphorus hungry
and on poor sandy soils an extra 8 oz a square yard (220 g a
square metre) of Gafsa rock phosphate is an advantage.
Veganic gardeners, or vegetarians who object to bonemeal, can
double the rock phosphate instead.

Royal Sovereign is still the finest early variety for flavour,
but Cambridge Rival has large fruit on erect stems clear of the
ground for wet seasons and resistance to redcore disease, as
well as a flavour not perfect but good. Follow it with Talisman,
upright and disease resisting and cropping over a long period;
Redgauntlet another heavy-cropping disease beater; and

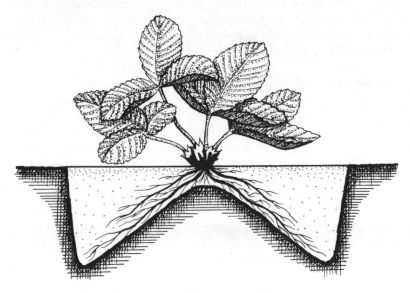

9 Strawberry planting

Cambridge Late Pine, to pick on into August with a delicious, almost a pineapple flavour and resistance to both mildew and frost.

Break up the clods, tread firm and rake level before planting in rows eighteen inches (45 cm) apart and a foot (30 cm) between plants, with a foot (30 cm) between the last row and the wire netting at the sides of the bed. Take out trowel holes four inches (10 cm) wide but shallower in the middle and set each rooted runner on top of this mound with its roots spread downwards; heap the soil over them, firming it back with the handle of the trowel. Strawberries are shallow rooting and need to have their roots spread wide and their growing points or 'crowns' on the surface. If they are all bunched into a dibber hole, frost can heave them right out of the ground and they start with a handicap. Pot-grown plants should be put without breaking the soil ball, but the crown level with the soil surface.

Hoe between the rows if the weeds grow fast in a mild autumn, and again in April before spreading a two-inch (5 cm) thick mulch of peat or leaf-mould to hold down annual weeds. One of the 'hastened' leaf-moulds will do, but not compost or mowings, because it is important not to use anything that attracts slugs. Straw, renewed each spring, is unattractive to slugs, but it is increasingly hard to get, for no organic farmer will sell what he needs for his land. Any other straw will have had a selective killer used on it, but MCPA, used in the spring of the year before harvest and spread the next spring, is allowed by the British Organic Standards as safe. It is also possible to buy ready-made strawberry mats which fit round the plants – these are excellent but more expensive.

As the young plants start to grow they will produce early flowers which should be nipped out to put more strength into later blossom and any stray runners should be removed. After the first spray with nicotine in April, spray with derris because you will be picking and eating the fruit. Mildew and grey mould are problems in some gardens, and dusting with flowers of sulphur is an answer. Where it is really bad, as it may be on cold, damp clays, grow Redgauntlet, which resists both. It has only a 'fair' flavour, but even that is better than no strawberries.

In the past it was usual to burn the straw and the leaves off the bed to get rid of disease and pest eggs, but the modern garden method is to clip the rows with shears at the end of the season, and take the clippings with the partly 1–1 rotted straw to the compost heap. In the spring scatter 4 oz a square yard (110g a square metre) of fine bonemeal (or dried sewage sludge if you can get it), and renew the peat or leaf-mould mulch, which will mainly have been taken under by the worms.

By the time each bed becomes ready to return to vegetable growing, it will be rich and productive with the unexpended portion of the year's rations from every season. This makes the six-bed rotation a permanent soil-enrichment programme, and suggests that on the four-bed system there should be four strawberry places on each.

12.

September

Prepare the vegetable store

There is no need to wait for the haulm to die down on the second early potatoes, for as soon as it starts to yellow it has ceased to fatten the tubers. Dig them with care and spread them on opened-out polythene bags to dry in the sun for forty-eight hours, then pick out the reproachful fork-speared accidents for immediate eating and store the rest in the paper sacks that are all we can buy or beg today. Think ahead to where the roots are going to go this year. It must be rat-proof, which rules out small-scale potato or root clamps outside, dark, and hold a temperature of about 35°F (2°C). These are exactly the conditions offered by the wine and other cellars under the large houses of the past. New houses today sit on thin concrete rafts, and it would be easy enough while the excavating machinery is there to scoop out a cellar and build something dark, cool and convenient for the kitchen.

Lining a shed with hardboard and fibreglass is a good investment, for deep freezes also cost time and fuel to prepare and blanch the roots that could store just as easily in tea-chests, with peat, fine ashes or sand to take care of the humidity. These can be covered with old blankets as light excluders if you use the easiest trick of all – a bayonet-type light socket on the wall, not only to switch on by the door to find the vegetables you need, but to take higher wattage bulbs (up to 250), or infra-red heater bulbs, for hard winters.

Available for eating	Family	Sowing	Planting
Beans (dried or frozen)	7	May-June	–
Beans, French	7	May	–
Beans, runner	7	–	May
Beet (fresh)	2	March	–
Cabbage	4	June	July
Carrots (summer)	12	March	–
Carrots (Shorthorn)	12	March	–
Cauliflowers	4	February	April
Cucumbers (outdoor)	5	April	–
Kale	4	April	June-July
Kohl rabi	4	March-April	–
Lamb's-lettuce	13	May	–
Landcress	4	May	–
Leeks	8	April	July
Lettuce	3	May	–
Marrows; Courgettes	5	April	–
Miner's lettuce	10	May	–
Onions	8	March	–
Onions (spring)	8	August	–
Peas (maincrop)	7	April	–
Potatoes (second early)	11	–	March
Pumpkins	5	April	May
Radishes	4	March-August	–
Spinach, New Zealand	1	March	–
Spinach (summer)	2	April	–
Sweetcorn (fresh)	6	April-May	–
Tomatoes (outdoor)	11	–	May

Heat insulation is valuable for keeping stored roots (and fruit) *cool* as well as frost-free. Place a thermometer to indicate maximum and minimum temperatures in your possible storage places as well as a hygrometer, which measures humidity. Both are useful tools for any gardener because it is useless growing good food only to waste it in storage. Potatoes and roots need 34-40°F (2-5°C) and 90-95 per cent humidity; apples and pears need the same temperature range but 80-90 per cent humidity, which was formerly supplied to a fruit room over the stables, from the warmth and breath of the horses. Today, humidity can be provided by saucers of water, as necessary, in an attic. Onions and garlic need to be cool and dry, 35-40°F (2-

5 °C) and 60-70 per cent humidity, which is attic temperature without saucers, or an unheated boxroom, while pumpkins and ripening green tomatoes need 50-60°F (10-15°C) and 60-70 per cent humidity. Move the max-min thermometer and hygrometer about to find the right conditions in all the places where you could fit fruit and vegetables without domestic disturbance, so you know where everything can go *before* it is time to harvest the crops.

The value of August and September room lies in there being still time for sowing with enough of the ebbing growth tide left for winter crops to succeed. Many gardeners concentrate on early and second early potatoes, with only a few Desiree, Record and Arran Consul maincrops that are dug in October, too late to sow anything but broad or daffa beans to follow them. There is still time for winter lettuce, spring onions and the other salad crops that provide a change for everyone and keep up the essential food supply for those on rotating allergy diets.

Sow green manure crops in September

Growing time is important for green manure crops, which are among the organic gardener's methods of conserving fertility and adding nitrogen and humus to the soil. The only time small gardens have for growing green manure crops is in winter when spare space that would otherwise grow weeds can grow fertility instead. Weeds, especially chickweed, can gather the last nitrogen of summer with other plant foods that winter rains wash away, but they cannot compete with farm crops bred to grow bulk fast for winter and early-spring grazing. There is also the important *garden* difference between crops and weeds. Most weeds have seeds that germinate over a period, with only a varied percentage coming up the first year however suitable the conditions, while others germinate at intervals like time bombs, so 'one year's weed – seven year's seed', the old gardener's saying, is quite literally true. Farm and garden varieties have had this ability bred out of them by selection through the centuries.

Perhaps the best plant-food holder for any soil is Hungarian grazing rye (not annual rye *grass* which is slower and less effective). This will grow about fifteen inches (38cm) tall from a late August or September sowing and eight (20cm) from mid-October, so it can still go in after maincrop potatoes. It offers not only a bulk of leaf to dig in, but a web of root hairs so thick that it is said that if all were joined together they would reach half a mile, as extra humus rapidly available for bacterial breakdown in spring.

Dig over the cleared ground, rake it fine and level and sow at the rate of an ounce a square yard (28g a square metre) like a very thin lawn. Another method that makes seed go further is to take out inch-deep (2.5cm) furrows with the hoe corner, four inches (10cm) apart and space the seeds along them at roughly three-inch (8cm) intervals, covering them afterwards with the hoe. A single-furrow, hand seed-drill, ideally second-hand and shared between neighbours, saves far more time than most garden gadgets and is a more useful buy for an organic gardeners' group or club than a far more costly compost chopper.

Dig in the rye before April ends, for if it grows on to tall green straw, the bacteria that decay it will increase so fast that they rob the next sown crops of nitrogen and phosphorus. Grazing rye, cut at the sappy, high-protein stage that farmers need it for stock, can be followed by potatoes or any other garden crop. Those who keep a goat can tether it on the rye and gain an increased milk yield and a happy goat (but less leaf), while still keeping the surface 'turf' and all the roots. Chickens will not eat rye.

However, rye merely holds on to the nitrogen that is already in the soil. Winter tares are pea-tribe plants which gather nitrogen from the air and add it to the soil. Sow these from August till the first week in October, in furrows like the rye and at the same spacing; as the seed is larger, one ounce (28g) sows 80 feet (24m) of row. This sowing will be ready to turn under in March or April, when, if the soil is poor and space can be spared, another sowing can be made to dig in when the buds first show in July. Unlike rye, winter tares are attractive to chickens whose instinct tells them that they do not have the bacteria to digest cellulose like goats and cattle so must have protein and carbohydrate. Birds, moved round the garden in an ark clearing weeds, can feed off tares and save their owner the job of turning the foliage under. The fibre the chickens do not digest will have gone back in their droppings to help the humus supply.

Undersown lawns beat birds

The September sowing of winter tares offers a way of starting a new lawn where the soil is poor and the sparrows are fierce.

Leave the crop until May or June when it will be in full flower, and then scatter your grass seed over the foliage. Brush and shake the foliage to make sure that all the grass seed reaches the ground. When you can see the grass is well up, set the mower as high as it will go and mow off the tares for compost material. This releases the hoarded nitrogen from them at grass-roots level and thickens up the new grass into a turf ready for autumn mowing. The tares are biennial and so die off when their job is done.

The best real clover for gardeners is the old Essex Red variety, *Trifolium pratense*, once sown with turnips after harvest on the stubble for sheep feed in spring on the South Downs of Sussex. It is cheaper than most green manures because the seeds are so tiny that one ounce (28g) sows ten square yards (or metres). This is why, though the Royal Horticultural Society has recommended it as a green manure since the 1900s, it is almost unknown to modern gardeners. The problem of sowing so little is solved by mixing each ounce (28g) thoroughly with half a pound (220g) of bonemeal and sowing the mixture on four square yards (or metres). The cream-coloured bonemeal against the dark soil shows clearly where you have been, and gives a 2oz a square yard (55g a square metre) dressing of organic phosphates and nitrogen to start the crop on a poor soil.

Green manure and poultry

Sow the clover on well-raked and levelled soil in August or September, ready to dig under in April when it will be up to a foot (30cm) high, which was when the sheep were folded on it. It is even better for starting a lawn under than tares, with the grass seed sown in April on top of the budding clover, which of course protects the seed from birds. If it does seed itself the seedlings are killed out by mowing, unlike the perennial white clover of most lawns.

The September sowing is much appreciated by chickens, and if the ark is moved every other day so the birds do not peck it too hard it will last from early April till June, with eggs as the 'spin off' from building fertility. For green manures build fertility, while compost-material crops, like those from weeds on waste land, or sunflowers sown after dug-in sanitation buckets or fresh poultry manure, spread it. Where there is ground to spare in a neglected garden, summer green manuring is a good way of improving the soil.

The best summer green manure, if you can spare the space, is the annual lupin *(Lupinus angustifolius)*, which not only has efficient nitrogen-fixing bacteria in its roots, but also symbiotic fungi that reach out and make phosphates available. It contains an alkaloid which makes the large seeds distasteful to birds, and rabbits dislike the foliage, both garden advantages, but it is not such a good weed suppressor as the other green manures.

Sow the seeds singly in dibber holes an inch (2.5cm) deep, six inches (15cm) apart and eight (20cm) between rows, in the first week in April. Let them grow on, hoeing between the rows to kill off weed seedlings, and mow them in July, planting Brussels sprouts in the undug soil. Another trick is to sow sweetcorn between the lupin rows in May after hoeing, and to leave the corn to take advantage of the nitrogen and the *phosphorus* gathered by the lupins which will be suppressed by the stronger and later crop. An April sowing of lupins can also be dug under in August, in time for planting a new strawberry bed.

Organic pest control in September
In September, check that the grease-band paint in the orchard has not dried up or become jammed with the two-way traffic of pests. The wingless females of the winter moth *(Cheimatobia brumata)* will be on the way up in the first week in October, so make sure the sticky band is ready for them on both apples and plums, The black-cherry aphid and the plum leaf-curling aphid, which have both been multiplying by unisex all the summer, now reach their sexual winged stage and as soon as the cherry and plum leaves fall, spray with nicotine and catch them with all the efficiency of killing queen wasps.

13.

October

October is the storing month, when the last of the roots for lifting come up with care to store in boxes because some, like carrots, keep better that way, and others for convenience, because digging slender scorzonera or tapered parsnips, like Tender and True, on a clay soil with fine snow blowing on the wind is not a task to linger over. If possible, leave roots in the ground, to save shed space, and be thankful that the cabbage tribe will take the worst our winters can fling at them, though American gardeners have to store even their broccoli in root cellars which are becoming increasingly rare in an age of home canning and deep freezing.

Peat is still the most popular storage medium, bought in bales, chopped down with a spade and watered, then shovelled to mix in the moisture, for it should not be too dusty dry or it will extract moisture from the vegetables. It is best to buy the peat well before lifting and leave it about three days after chopping to get it just moist enough to be thirsty. The problem of using fine ashes from solid-fuel central heating is that although these are mostly silica and alumina (unlike high-potash woodstove ashes) and cost nothing, they are inclined to get the roots too dry. Beet, carrots, swedes and turnips should all store in containers with the chosen medium spread in a layer on the bottom, and the roots set out in it with about a half-inch (1 cm) gap all round each. Then add more peat or ashes to allow a clear inch (2.5 cm) of the medium before the next layer of roots goes in.

Available for eating	Family	Sowing	Planting
Beans, French	7	May	–
Beans, runner	7	–	May
Beet (fresh)	2	March	–
Cabbage	4	June	July
Carrots (early)	12	March	–
Carrots (maincrop)	12	April	–
Cauliflowers	4	February	April
Celery	12	March-April	May-June
Kale	4	April	June-July
Kohl rabi	4	March-April	–
Lamb's-lettuce	13	May	–
Landcress	4	May	–
Leeks	8	April	July
Lettuce	3	May	–
Marrows; Courgettes	5	April	–
Miner's lettuce	10	May	–
Onions	8	March	–
Onions (spring)	8	August	–
Parsnips	12	February-March	–
Peas (maincrop)	7	April	–
Potatoes (maincrop)	11	–	April-May
Pumpkins	5	April	May
Radishes	4	March-August	–
Salsify	3	March	–
Scorzonera	3	March	–
Spinach, New Zealand	1	March	–
Spinach (summer)	2	April	–
Sweetcorn (fresh)	6	April-May	–
Tomatoes (outdoor)	11	–	May

Real tea-chests are increasingly scarce and sell expensively for packing crockery and books on moving days. One way round the problem is to collect the white plastic, one-gallon (or 4 litre) liquid containers (such as those holding shampoos and setting fluids used by ladies' hairdressers) and saw off the tops. These containers are oblong and about a foot (30cm) high and though they are on the small side and use rather more peat proportionately, there is no risk of root rot spreading and no need to delve in deep peat to find the bottom layers. Select the contents which will probably be about as many as you would normally fetch and fill the container as suggested. Pack these together in a tea-chest size block, and put the next layer set across them, so they bond together like a brick wall without toppling over. As the containers are translucent white, cover them with an old blanket to exclude light.

Potato storage

Potatoes breathe much more than other roots and therefore need no peat or ashes. Ideally they should go in jute sacks, but they would store just as well in the plastic containers, provided these were covered with blankets or something thick to exclude the light. The essentials are to keep their temperature above the minimum 35 °F (2 °C) and to avoid the greenness from exposure to light that shows the presence of the alkaloid solanine. Frosted potatoes develop a most unpleasant, sweetish taste, which can be removed by putting them in a temperature of 60-65 °F (15-18 °C) for several days. Solanine can produce symptoms like gastric influenza if green potatoes are eaten in quantity, and in quite small amounts by those who are extra sensitive.

Seed potatoes are not harmed by exposure to light, which, in fact, improves them by increasing sprouting, but care should be taken to cover any exposed tubers when earthing up or when growing on the 'no-dig' system. It takes long exposure to light to turn potatoes green and this process can be reversed by storing them in complete darkness until they return to normal. In the USA, with a warmer and longer 'fall' than our often wet and cold autumns, they spread out newly harvested potatoes in layers one-spud thick in a sheltered place away from rain and wind at a temperature of 60-65 °F (15-18 °C) for a week and then turn them over to give the other sides a turn. This is called 'curing' and is intended to thicken their skins, heal any grazes or scratches from lifting and improve the keeping qualities of maincrops and second earlies for storing. Potatoes show the greatest difference between organically and chemically grown, so it is worth taking trouble to store them as carefully as apples. We could try the American curing method easily in an empty conservatory or sunny spare room.

Green tomato ripening

Green tomatoes also need care, for each is as alive as a fertile egg, and in our climate we can easily have four times as much of the crop left unripe as we have eaten red and ripe. Tomatoes contain fruit acids that tenderize meat as well as being a useful supply of vitamins and minerals for soups and stews right round the year, and are one of our most useful storing crops. Set out the green fruit in paper-lined chitting trays, on their sides and not touching each other, and cover them with oblongs of dressing-gown wadding, which is rather cheaper than cotton-wool and should last for years. Lift the trays off the stack once a week, remove the wadding (which will not catch on the stalks as these are sideways), pick out the ripe ones for cooking or bottling, and replace it.

This system will keep tomatoes ripening slowly into January, but with Harbinger, or any other fast ripener, most will come on fast enough on the plant to bottle or freeze before decay sets in. If frost merely threatens, pick all full-sized fruit from pale pink to cream in colour, and leave the smaller sizes unpicked for another week or ten days. Ripening on the plants makes all the difference to the taste, and real tinies never come to much in the end.

Apple storage
Apples need to have their stems left on, and the strictest attention paid to the period in season of every variety. Because no gardener can afford a cold store or a gas-tight room to pump full of carbon-dioxide, we have to ripen as they did in the past, handicapped by our lack of horses.

The ideal apple storage temperature is 32°F (0°C) with 80-90 per cent humidity, and at 40°F (5°C) they will only keep half as long. If the storage room is well insulated, and you have an old refrigerator that is still working (or can 'lend' yourself your own), put it in during the day time with its door open and cool the room down to give the newly picked apple harvest a good cold start. Shrivelling is caused by too low humidity or too high a temperature. It pays to have a length of old blanket hanging in a jam-jar of water to keep up the humidity for all the storage areas. The old idea of wrapping each apple in newspaper worked by keeping the air next to the skin saturated with the moisture the apple itself breathed out. The problem is that unwrapping and rewrapping every apple in the trays is so slow that it is done too seldom to discard any that are rotting off and spreading spores. Going through the trays quickly once a week when you select for eating, means that it is done in time.

Starting a herb bed

Like orchards, herb beds are planned ahead, and October is a good month for dividing up the perennials, especially mint *(Mentha spicata)* and its many sub-species and varieties to be found in any herb catalogue. Collect plastic honey or ice-cream containers, and melt small holes in the bottoms, fill them with garden soil and sink them in the herb bed. This method enables you to grow a collection of assorted mints while keeping them from swarming through each other.

A herb bed is outside the rotation, and is ideally sited near the kitchen door, for nipping out and snipping just a sprig of something. It needs careful digging to remove all perennial weeds, but no special manuring, for all herds produce the best flavours on poor soils. Nearly all of our herbs come from the dry, Mediterranean countries and they are easily overfed. Pot marjoram *(Origanum onites)* and thyme *(Thymus vulgaris* or the lemon-scented *T. citriodorus)* can both be divided in October, but the best way to obtain herbs is to raise them from seed, sown in April in labelled part-rows.

There is such a demand for herbs that the surplus seedlings can be sold off at fetes for worthy causes (after replanting when they are large enough to handle, three inches (8cm) apart each way) or potted on in yogurt cartons for sale. Young plants from seed last and yield far better than divisions torn off large clumps. The following are all good standard herbs to use in soups, salads and general cookery. The natural orders of each are given, so that people with allergies can use them as flavours, though their common characteristic is strongly tasting alkaloids or essential oils and these cannot provide a real contribution to any diet.

Balm or **lemon balm** *(Melissa officinalis: Labiatae)* is fully hardy, but comes up more slowly than the others in this easy group.

Basil *(Ocimum minimum: Labiatae)* is a half-hardy annual described earlier.

Burnet *(Sanguisorba minor: Rosaceae)* is a perennial, used to give a slightly cucumber flavour to salads or as a tea.

Chervil *(Anthriscus cerefolium: Umbelliferae)* is an annual that runs to seed fast like spinach, but should be sown thinly in rows eight inches (20cm) apart, thinned to six (15cm) between plants, and snipped off just above the root six to eight weeks after the first sowing in March. This will provide another cut, but leave some of the first to run to seed – providing some for a July sowing and some for the following year. It is used in soups and salads, and freezes better than it dries.

Chives *(Allium schoenoprasum: Liliaceae)* is a small, perennial onion to snip for leaves to flavour almost anything. Increase by dividing the clumps in March or April. It can be raised from seed but rarely is because it is so prolific that it edges kitchen-garden beds.

Fennel *(Foeniculum vulgare: Umbelliferae)* grows very large and strong. Sow seed in pinches about eight inches (20cm) apart in a colony of four, and thin to the best. This is the tallest herb and should go at the back of the bed for leaves to use in sauces, soups and salads, and seeds to gather for a tea.

Rosemary *(Rosemarinus officinalis: Labiateae)* is an evergreen shrub that grows best in shelter on the south side of a house because it is not fully hardy. A sprig of rosemary can be added to the water when cooking peas or potatoes and placed inside roasting birds. It can be raised easily from seed sown like the others, but those who wish to take a 'Rosemary for Remembrance' from a friend, should break off a 6-9 inch (15-20cm) length shoot *downwards* so it has a 'heel' of the parent branch, in June, July or August, and stand this in a jam-jar full of water. In a few weeks it will grow small, white roots, and can be planted in a sunny place and watered to give it a start.

Sage *(Salvia officinalis: Labiatae)* is easily raised from seed sown in April, but slow to germinate and therefore worth marking with radishes like parsnips. Thin to six inches (15cm) apart and expect to raise fresh every three years for it is much easier from seed than cuttings.

Summer Savoury *(Satureia hortensis: Labiatae)* is an annual with a taste rather like sage, excellent in stuffing and soups as well as for adding flavour to some of the rather dull bean dishes in vegetarian diets. Sow it like chervil and take two cuts a year from an April and a July sowing.

All herbs are at their best for drying when the flowers are just starting to open, so cut the foliage then and hang in bunches with a brown paper bag over each and head downwards, to dry slowly indoors. When they are crisp, put them through a mincing machine if you want them in fine fragments, stalks and all, or rub them through your fingers before storing in screw-topped jars.

Organic fruit care in October

October starts the leaf season, and every organic gardener should gather all he can from our most wasted humus source. In orchards, however, about 85 per cent of the spores of apple scab overwinter on fallen leaves. One way to deal with these is by running a rotary lawn-mower over them as they lie so that the worms can take them right under, instead of just as far as their stalks. This is effective in grassed-down orchards, but otherwise sweep and gather the leaves and tuck them away into one of the 'hastened' heaps.

October gives a chance to catch the apple sucker *(Psylla mali)* when it has just arrived to lay eggs that will hatch to small and lively creatures that eat apple blossom and can destroy whole crops if they are allowed to build up a population. Spray with nicotine and soft soap if you had blossom damage or even something eating the young leaves round the trusses last spring.

Raspberry pruning

It is also raspberry-pruning time. Cut the temporary ties that have held the young shoots growing since the fruited canes were removed, and choose the best five or six on each plant. Tie these

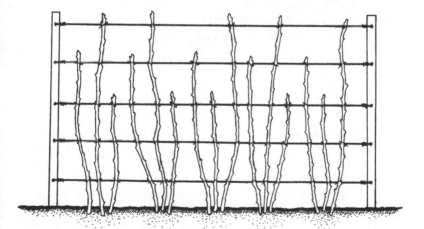

10 Raspberry pruning

to the wires, shortening them so they finish at three different lengths, to avoid crowding the blossom which is often at the ends, and remove the smaller canes completely. Then dig between the rows, turning under the grass and comfrey mulch, removing any canes that are growing between the rows, and give your local robins their first chance at the raspberry-beetle chrysalids. Dig again in January if you have time.

Planting and pruning of cane fruit
October is as good a month as November for raspberry planting, either for a bed in a new garden, or renewing an old one, for raspberries and blackcurrants only last twelve to fifteen years, unlike the twenty to thirty years for red and white currants or gooseberries. Choose an equally sunny site in another part of the garden, and dig in compost or manure generously, plus 8 oz a square yard (220g a square metre) of bonemeal to start the bed away well. Space is more important than manure, for raspberries are shallow rooters and can take the plant foods and humus they need from surface mulches between their canes, but suffer if they are crammed closer together than their minimum of four feet (1 m 30) between rows and a foot (30 cm) between canes. If the rows go closer they will block the light from each other and the bees need sunlight to work the blossoms. If possible, site your rows in a north to south direction, so the sunlight falls *along* them, rather than only on the one lucky unshaded row that faces south.

Because raspberries root shallowly, and gather their food from the manure spread between the rows, they need only three-inch (8 cm) deep trenches, about spade width with foot-deep (30 cm) holes each end to hold their support posts which should be about six feet (2 m) long, with two cross-pieces nailed across the bottom of each. Make these a foot (30 cm) long and two inches (5 cm) wide, and creosote them, and the posts, thoroughly. Nail one cross-piece at the bottom on the side away from the row, and one a foot higher up, *facing* the row. Drill the posts to take the wire. Five wires are enough, and they serve to hold up the canes, however tall and heavy they become. Blackberries, loganberries and boysenberries all lie on their wires more heavily than raspberries, and need the same type of support system. If plain posts without cross-pieces are used, the weight of the canes will simply draw them together, but as the cross-pieces push in both directions (see diagram) they will stay firm for the life of the bed.

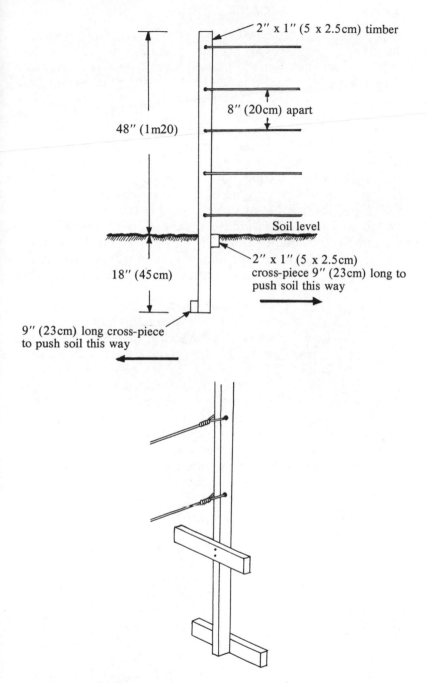

2″ x 1″ (5 x 2.5cm) timber

48″ (1m20)

8″ (20cm) apart

Soil level

18″ (45cm)

2″ x 1″ (5 x 2.5cm)
cross-piece 9″ (23cm) long to
push soil this way

9″ (23cm) long cross-piece
to push soil this way

11 Supporting posts for raspberry wires

Lloyd George is the last of the old raspberry varieties and it can be either an early July cropper, pruned as described, or left unpruned and cut down to ground level in March or April to fruit in September and October the following year. September, Hailsham and Lord Lambourne are also autumn fruiting, but never as popular as the ordinary summer kinds, because there is rarely enough sun to bring out their flavour.

The raspberries that have driven out the old kinds are the Malling varieties, bred by the late Norman Grubb of East Malling Research Station. The best of the mid-June fruiters is Malling Exploit with very large, well-flavoured berries. Malling Enterprise follows Lloyd George, and is another fine, large-flavoured kind, while Malling Landmark is the latest of all, beating Norfolk Giant on crop and flavour. Today the breeding effort is going into varieties that will grow without staking, for machine picking, but the older generation will last for the pick-it-yourself trade.

Raspberry canes are usually shaped like 'L's when they arrive, with the short arm the root. Place this along the three-inch (8cm) deep trench, fill in the soil, firm it well and tie the cane to the wires. This must not be allowed to fruit, but should be cut to six-inch (15cm) height in May before it blossoms, because its function is to produce the leaves that feed the young canes which will be growing ready to tie in next August and prune the following October. Leaving the new canes to fruit will be such a strain on the plants that it will be two more years before the bed produces a crop worth picking.

Before tying in the young canes on the loganberries and boysenberries, look round the bases of the thornless varieties (which are the best), and cut off any *thorned* shoots, for these can take the strength of the plant like suckers from the briar at the base of a rose. Do not shorten the main new shoots, for they will produce blossom bunches along their whole length, but tie them to cover the whole support structure. Leave room at the bottom of the structure for tying in the young shoots that will grow next summer ready to train up as replacements. If any of these trail very low, remove about six leaves a foot (30cm) up from the growing point, and place a brick where the leaves were. The shoot should root into the soil ready for removal to grow another plant for extending the soft-fruit beds.

The best flavoured blackberry is Himalayan Giant, but it is strong, very thorny and fruits as they all do on the old and young wood, but not at all on the inside of the tangle that they struggle to become. The best time to prune them is December, because by then they will have dropped all their leaves and it is possible to see what you are doing and to do it with thick gardening gloves and stout secateurs. The best of the easy thornless kinds, which are small enough to fit on the same type of supports used for raspberries and loganberries, is Oregon Cutleaf Thornless, a sport off the old parsley-leafed variety.

The trailing berries need richer feeding than raspberries, and after clearing perennial weed roots from the two-foot (60cm) wide strip along which they should be planted, dig in a pound (450g) of bonemeal and a pound (450g) of hoof and horn to every six feet (2m) of this strip. Set the posts six feet (2m) apart, and plant one loganberry, boysenberry or thornless blackberry in each. If you decide to have a Himalayan Giant, plant it by the central post and give it six feet (2m) to spread along on each side. Shorten all the long shoots on the new plants to fifteen inches (38cm), or just enough length to tie them to the lowest wires. Cut these out when the new shoots from their bases are all well established and tie these in ready to fruit next year.

When the blackberries are bare, begin by cutting out any dead or really old branches that are crowding the younger shoots. Cut these out in sections, threading them out between the young shoots. When there is some room clear, train in the long smooth 1–1 barked shoots that grew this summer, and tie them in. Some of the weaker of these will have to come out too, and in this case cut them through two inches (5cm) below the surface, which gives a thornless 'handle' by which to pull out the thorny monsters. Bush-fruit prunings are among the items that should *never* be composted. Burn them, not only because of the thorns, but because they may contain pest eggs.

Mid-October sees the last green-manure seed sowings. It should also see the last of the spring-cabbage plantings, with April, or the old Flower of Spring going out on this square of the rotation.

14.

November

In November, the last sowings of the year are longpod broad and daffa beans for stored protein, not only to save time in the crowded spring, and give an earlier crop, but because there is some control of blackfly *(Aphis fabae)*, due to the fact that the rather harder bark from the more mature growth makes only the tips attractive to the aphids, and these can be pinched out. This effect can be reinforced by sowing the beans on extra firm ground. Use a steel-shod dibber and plant without digging where autumn broccoli came out, or where the ground was trodden hard between outdoor tomato rows. With many of these time-honoured tricks we can only learn how good they are when we miss them for a season.

Birds against pests
The equally time-worn idea of hanging up fat over the roses to attract the tits in winter to eat the hibernating greenfly round the bases of the bushes, was tested at Long Ashton Research Station with apple trees, and reported in the *Annals of Applied Biology* (1978; 90, 133-46). They kept the tits off from the trees with netting held away from the trunks with metal hoops, and found that 82 per cent of the hibernating codling-moth larvae came through the winter successfully on these birdless trees, but only 48 per cent survived where the tits could get at them.

Smooth-barked young trees offer fewest hibernation oppor-

Available for eating	Family	Sowing	Planting
Beans (dried or frozen)	7	May-June	–
Beet (fresh)	2	March	–
Cabbage	4	June	July
Carrots (early)	12	March	–
Carrots (maincrop)	12	April	–
Cauliflowers	4	February	April
Celery (self-blanching)	12	March-April	May-June
Kale	4	April	June-July
Kohl rabi	4	March-April	–
Lamb's-lettuce	13	June-July	–
Landcress	4	July-August	–
Leeks	8	April	July
Miner's lettuce	10	June-July	–
Onions	8	March	–
Parsnips	12	February-March	–
Peas (dried or frozen)	7	January-May	–
Potatoes (maincrop)	11	–	April-May
Pumpkins (stored)	5	April	May
Radishes	4	March-August	–
Radish, Chinese	4	July	–
Salsify	3	March	–
Scorzonera	3	March	–
Spinach, New Zealand	1	March	–
Spinach (summer)	2	April	–
Sweetcorn (frozen)	6	April-May	–
Tomatoes (bottled)	11	–	May

tunities and those with thick trunks and plentiful crevices are the most likely to gain by a policy of fat-hanging. Some entomologists think that if gardeners made tit-fat hanging a tradition from Guy Fawkes' Day to New Year's Day, the result would be a neglect of duty by modern tits, who would feed on the fat rather than sleeping pests and eggs. Others (equally well qualified) consider that though fat provides hydro-carbons of value to small birds in hard weather, pests provide protein, and all insectivorous birds struggle to find themselves a balanced diet. So after a good feed of fat, the local tits would be protein-hungry and attack the pests with renewed vigour – especially when they learn that fruit trees mean fat as fast as they did pecking through milk-bottle tops to enjoy the cream.

November is the month for pruning and planting, digging in manure where trees and bush fruit will need it, rather than leaving land rough dug for the frost to break down, for research has shown that more plant foods are wasted by washing out of bare ground on sandy soil than we gain by leaving clays rough dug for frost.

Planting and pruning blackcurrants

Blackcurrants are the best value for Vitamin C from small gardens for the least trouble. Though Table 13 showed that Baldwin is highest, Westwick Choice comes a good second with 235mg per 100g, and also resists big-bud mite, while Wellington XXX (third with 204) is a heavy cropper famous for flavour. Both have about a three-week picking season (spreading the bottling period), with Westwick Choice later, and neither blossoms early enough to catch the worst frosts like the largest fruiting kind of all, Laxton's Giant, which is rare because so few people take the frost risk. Both are strong-growing kinds and are best planted five feet (1 m 50) apart each way to give plenty of room for picking. For very small gardens that can only spare three feet (1 m) apart, choose Amos Black,

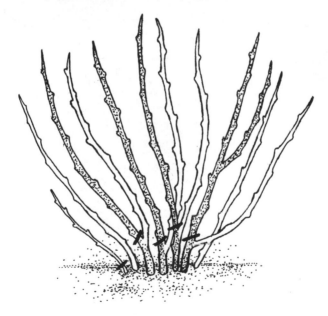

12 Blackcurrant – winter pruning

which is upright and small, fruiting late and well, but with rather more acid flavour than the first two.

Blackcurrants are nitrogen-greedy – therefore start them with manure rather than compost and as much as 2 lb a square yard (1 kg a square metre) of hoof and horn if you have none. This is to give them a starting stock, for in small gardens it pays to diet your blackcurrants by keeping them to comfrey, mowings and leaf-mould on the surface in moderation, for chemicals, especially nitrogen, put their weight up so they grow out of our small gardens. Dig their holes six inches (15 cm) deep and wide enough to spread their roots flat in a disc, and firm the soil over these, ensuring that it comes up as far as the soil mark on the stem that shows how deep they were planted in the nursery.

Then cut back the shoots with light-brown bark that grew in the past summer to three or four buds – whichever points away from the centre. There will be no fruit next summer, which will be spent growing strong shoots from these buds, and these will fruit all the way up the following year.

They fruit best on this young wood, which should be left full length, also on the two-year-old branches. In November,

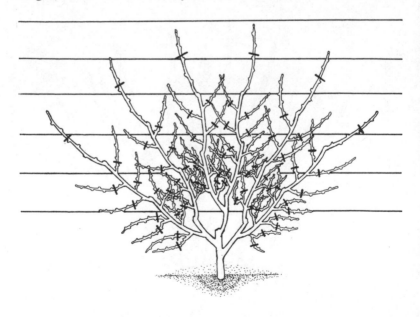

13 Redcurrant fan – winter pruning

remove about a third of the red-brown, barked branches that grew the previous summer and cut out any that are weak, or long and straggling, so they grow more long, straight shoots.

Red and white currants

Red and 'white' currants fruit on the old wood, like apples. Take back all the side shoots to three or four buds and shorten the leaders by about a third. This policy is all right for the first three prunings, but it means that the bushes grow bigger and bigger, so remove the longest and most straggling shoots each year, as though they were blackcurrants, to start more light-grey-barked young shoots low on the bushes.

Laxton's No.1, which is early, and Red Lake for later are both strong-growing kinds with a good flavour, while Versailles is the last of the white varieties still in cultivation. The best way to grow them is trained up a wall, so they can be protected by a nylon net, and grown in beds too narrow for anything else. Trained or cordon currant canes are very expensive today, but it is easy to grow your own.

Select the best of the young shoots that grew the previous summer on the pruned-off branches, cut them off with a 'heel' of older wood, and shorten them if they are longer than a foot (30cm); eight inches (20cm) or six inches (15cm) is about the best length. Make a cut with a spade along a garden line, insert the cuttings along it two inches (5cm) apart and four (10cm) deep, and tread the soil firmly back. They are rooted and growing by the following autumn, ready to cut back to six buds and transplant at a foot (30cm) spacing. By the second autumn they will be ready for their permanent homes against the wall.

Shorten the new shoots only by about a quarter of their length, to the first strong bud that points along the wall, and take off any others that point away from it to the lowest along the wall-pointing one. The next year they will produce a few bunches of currants, and some side shoots. Pinch out their tips in July to put more strength into the fruiting buds round their bases, and when the leaves fall in November cut them back to about an inch (25cm) length, shortening the leaders by 25 per cent. Wall redcurrants are uncommon, but they will live for many years, fruiting freely on the old wood providing they are pruned hard and trained flat, so the sun can ripen the wood for fruiting. It cannot ripen in the middle of an overgrown mass.

Black, red and white currants all need the same manuring,

but the last two should have even less nitrogen, for giving in to the greed of your currants makes them more liable to attack by *Septoria ribis*, the leaf-spot fungus which can make the leaves start falling in June and July in wet summers, with fruit withering. If this happens, spray with Burgundy mixture in November. The fungus spores winter on fallen currant leaves, and as all three can only be forked over very shallowly because of their shallow roots, water the fallen leaves with urine on the apple-scab principle. This will not give too much nitrogen, because it will all be spent by the time the roots are feeding again.

14 Gooseberry pruning

Gooseberry planting and pruning

Gooseberries can also be trained up walls, either on a single stem, or 'cordon' – which allows room for perhaps a dozen kinds for those who are starting a gooseberry collection, or fan trained. They are, however, so prickly that the hard pruning they need becomes a burden. They fruit on the old wood like redcurrants, and need the same soil treatment, but with the addition of a pound a square yard (450g a square metre) of rock potash on sandy soils. This newly available mineral is the answer to the problem of growing gooseberries in Rhododendron and heather-type gardens in Surrey, but on clays they do well with comfrey if they run low. The symptoms of potash hunger in gooseberries are leaves turning a blue-green, with light-brown edges that look as though they have been scorched.

The main gooseberry problem is weeding under the bushes and Careless, the commonest kind, seems to be so named because it does not care how badly it scratches its owner. Choose Whitesmith instead, which is upright, resists American gooseberry mildew, and fruits rather earlier, ripening to amber yellow, or Langley Gage, equally resistant and upright, green ripening to cream with the finest flavour of all. For a red kind, with flavour, upright habit and mildew resistance, buy Bedford Red, which is the tastiest, but has a smaller crop. These three are the best of the two-hundred-odd known gooseberries rapidly being driven out of cultivation by Careless, which is large fruited, heavy cropping and so savage that some day gooseberry pickers' strikes may drive it off the market.

Plant the bushes four feet (1m30) apart each way, six inches (15cm) deep and the roots spread like those of blackcurrants, with the soil well firmed. Order your bushes early, and offer to pay extra for specimens with extra long 'legs'. A gooseberry's leg is the length of brown trunk from where the roots spread to the first branches, and the longer it is the more room there will be to reach under the weeding. After planting, cut back the light-brown barked shoots to between three and five buds, which gives scope to choose one that points up and away from the centre as the end one, which will grow a new shoot rather than blossom.

In the November after planting, shorten these new shoots to about eight inches (20cm) long and take out completely any that are growing towards the middle. The best shape for a gooseberry bush is that of an empty ice-cream cone, and this is easy enough if you buy an upright variety and train it so the sun can get into the middle to ripen the wood and the fruit and you can reach in to pick it without bloodshed.

Cherries on walls

The best place for cherries in modern gardens in trained on walls away from the vandalism of modern birds, and a nylon net curtain is cheaper than a fruit cage for cherries hung with snow. The cherry problem is that most sweet, eating varieties need pollen partners, and few houses have enough window-free wall for more than one.

Morello, the easy, hardy, cooking kind, can train on a north or even an east wall, and is completely self-fertile. Though the Duke cherries sometimes fruit alone, this is chancy and they are not very sweet. The new Canadian variety, Stella, the first self-fertile sweet cherry and which has strong and solid branches, is the answer. Buy one as a 'maiden', which is a year-old tree, and cut the main leader out after planting in November, with care to protect the cut with Arbortect, or one of the other modern plastic paints to keep out dieback or other spores. Then train the small side branches along the wall, tying them back to the vine eyes (like big screweyes) in rawlplugs that should hold the faulty telephone wire which is best for training all fruit, for the insulation is softer than the thin plastic on 'garden wire', which rubs through bark and causes canker.

During the summer tie any side shoots to the wires and pinch back any that point out, or any that race up fast from low on the tree, to buds that point along the wall. Cherries fruit most on one- and two-year-old wood, so do not need spur-pruning like apples. Cut out broken or sickly branches, or those that have ceased to fruit; otherwise stick to dieback removal, and pinching or snipping soft shoots in summer and tying in. If you have room for two cherries, plant Bigarreau Napoleon and Frogmore Early, both red and yellow and fruiting in June and July. They have large blossom which makes a fine show against a red brick wall.

Plum programme

Plums are also good wall fruit and, like cherries, will fruit on north or east walls, leaving the south and west for peaches, apricots or nectarines. Oullin's Golden Gage is self-fertile, and so is Czar, but only a cooker or bottler. If there is room on an east wall, plant Coe's Golden Drop and Count d'Althan's Gage, both delicious golden plums to eat in September. Kirke's Blue, reputedly the finest-flavour plum, needs a south wall, or a southern garden, and Cambridge Gage, perhaps the best-flavoured greengage of all, as a pollen partner.

Two feet (60cm) is about the minimum width for a stone-fruit border, for this allows space to dig out a trench to hold lasting plant foods. Make this three feet (1m) long, two (60cm) deep and eighteen inches (45cm) wide, bringing it out clear of any concrete foundations. Fortunately, stone fruit have relatively weak roots compared with poplars and do not creep under the house into subsoil. A good supply of slowly available food keeps the roots at home if they have any tendency to wander.

Take out any builder's rubbish you find and wheel it away with the subsoil, which is the main reason for digging so deep. Then mix 4lb (2kg) of bonemeal and 6lb (3kg) of oystershell chicken grit (except on chalk soils) and scatter about half this on the bottom of the hole, tread in firmly six inches (15cm) of good garden soil, add the rest of the mixture and then fill in with more good garden soil. If the soil is very bad, buy a few lawn turves (which will have good loam under them and be quite cheap if fetched from a garden centre) and pack them, grass down, in the bottom of the hole.

Keep the trunk of the trained tree away from the wall, so it is possible to get a syringe behind it, and above all do not forget to keep the bed level well below the damp course. Grease-banding is not easy on trained trees, because ants and many other creatures simply walk up the wall. The answer is to paint a strip of grease-band material along the wall, not right round the house but below the trees.

It is expensive to use a modern tree-grease on this scale, so the following old-fashioned recipe for a do-it-yourself grease is suggested. Mix together eight parts of powdered resin, four parts linseed oil, four parts turpentine and half a part of honey; bring the mixture slowly to boiling point, and paint it on the wall while still hot.

The easiest stone fruit for any wall is the red cherry-plum, and its yellow variety. Both are self-fertile, with fruit about the size of nutmegs and the disadvantage of cropping very well one year and missing the next. These plums were once grown for the tall hedges that sheltered Somerset cider orchards, planted three feet (1m) apart, with stakes between each and woven into a kind of basket work by the hedgers. If cherry-plums can be found (there are firms that stock them still), prune merely by removing dieback, and tie the shoots into the wires to ripen their wood and its fruit behind a nylon net. It is the only stone fruit that can be cut back carelessly, and it has even been pruned by farmworkers with long hedging bills as issued to the Somerset Home Guard in 1940 as well as Monmouth's men. It bottles well, makes jam, and is sweet when ripe; larger than a cherry, much smaller than a greengage, and unfamiliar to modern greengrocers and housewives.

Damsons also make a hedge, but again the problem is that the birds strip the buds before you have hardly even seen the blossom. Farleigh is the hedge damson, to plant three feet (1m) apart and crowd itself tall like a Leyland Cypress *(Cupressus leylandii)*, the fastest evergreen hedge which only gives gardeners satisfaction till its fifteenth year, when it is too big for anything but firewood. Treat Farleigh as a hedge, clipping back the bare branches in November, and chancing the loss of the crop Merryweather is also self-fertile and can be trained on a wall (with a fruit net to protect it) by those who like damsons, which are on the sharp side but excellent for wine and damson cheese.

All stone fruits need lime, because the bulk of their stones is calcium, and the rest is very largely potash, but their deep roots keep up the supply. They can become short of nitrogen, yielding small fruit, with larger stones than normal, which is a sign that they need deep-litter poultry compost or any other manure, spread beneath – but not touching – the trees. Those who can plant standard plums should choose bush specimens of self-fertile Victoria, or Kirke's Blue, with Belle de Louvaine, its other good pollinator. Make the holes two feet (60cm) square and deep; drive the stout stakes a foot (30cm) deep in the bottom of the holes, and fit the roots round them, for if stakes are driven in after planting they may damage the roots.

15.

December

The year ends with time to plan ahead and look through the diary that every gardener should keep, to see what went wrong and what went right, of what we grew too little and what we sowed too late. Some of us may decide to give up maincrop potatoes because they are easily bought. Others feel that freshness, flavour and freedom from pesticides are all-important and that it is better to grow the maximum quantities of the bulky vegetables that include potatoes as well as salads right round the year, even if we have to slaughter the shrubs and abolish the lawn. We dug it up for Victory once – we could dig it up now for healthier food.

It is likely that as allergies increase with rising pollution from pesticides, fumes and increasing numbers of additives, many more of the unfortunate people who are sensitive to even traces of these substances will form co-operatives through which those of them who have no gardens can be sure of getting what their health demands. In Switzerland these are already working successfully, with members paying a fixed annual sum for vegetables round the year; this covers the costs of including gardeners' wages, and works out at about wholefood shop prices – far less than for any individual employing a gardener to grow the family supply.

The Henry Doubleday Research Association publishes a directory of organic farmers, market gardeners and other organically grown produce suppliers, but bought foods cannot

Available for eating	Family	Sowing	Planting
Artichokes, Jerusalem	3	–	February-March
Beans (dried or frozen)	7	May-June	–
Beet (stored)	2	May	–
Beet (leaf)	2	April	–
Broccoli (heading)	4	May	July
Brussels sprouts	4	May	June-July
Cabbage	4	June	July
Carrots (stored)	12	May	–
Celeriac	12	March	May
Celery	12	March-April	May-June
Hamburg parsley	12	March-April	–
Kale	4	April	June-July
Lamb's-lettuce	13	July-August	–
Landcress	4	August-September	–
Leeks	8	April	July
Lettuce	3	March-July	–
Miner's lettuce	10	July-August	–
Onions (stored)	8	March	–
Parsnips	12	February-March	–
Peas (dried or frozen)	7	January-May	–
Potatoes (stored)	11	–	April-May
Pumpkins	5	April	May
Radish, Chinese	4	July	–
Salsify	3	March-April	–
Scorzonera	3	March-April	–
Spinach (winter)	2	September	–
Swedes (stored)	4	July	–
Sweetcorn (frozen)	6	April-May	–
Tomatoes (bottled)	11	–	May-June
Turnips (stored)	4	June-July	–

be as cheap as growing as much of your own food as possible. The major problem is one of running an alternative food distribution system to the mammoth chain of markets, processors and wholesalers that carry the products of factory farms and agribusiness enterprises to the supermarkets. This is not insoluble, however, because not only is small beautiful, it can be vastly cheaper in many ways. Organic growers in many areas are organizing 'consumers' clubs' where produce can be brought to a central depot and collected, for few smallholders can . spare the time to stand at market-stalls waiting for customers.

Today we live at the end of food chains that reach right round the world. We expect to be able to eat oranges, lemons, bananas and apples every day of our lives without thought of season or distance. There is no way in which we can build up an alternative apple-chain fast enough from New Zealand, South Africa, Tasmania and Canada to replace sprayed fruit with unsprayed. We shall have to return to enjoying our own apples and pears in their seasons, as each kind comes to perfection, taking also what the organic growers of the world can offer us.

Of course this depends on whether we can pay for it, for the cost gap between 'battery fruit' – pruned by spraying, fed by chemicals and harvested, graded and packed by machine – and the 'hand-grown' product from an organic orchard, will grow ever wider. More and more it is going to pay us to grow our own fruit.

We have here another variation of the potato problem. If we have small gardens, should we give up the major part of our room to growing enough apples to keep 0.3 per cent of a doctor away every day, or should we concentrate on fresh salads, carrots (which are the most heavily sprayed of all the vegetable factory products) or potatoes with which you really tell the difference by the flavour?

The answer is a matter of taste, space and personal choice in the only area in our lives in which all our choices can be purely personal. We can, if we wish, plant the banners of an ever-growing army of apples that are important because they are our own. Let us sound the first blast of the trumpet against the monstrous regiment of Golden Delicious, and its polythene-skinned, sugared-water-blooded, paint-bright partners. The important fact about Cox is not that is has a short name everyone knows and it sells well if it is packed, graded and marketed well; it is that Mr Richard Cox (1776-1845) of Lawn Cottage, Colnbrook, Slough, a retired brewer, grew it from a pip he sowed *in his own garden.* The tree itself blew down in 1911, but its grafting wood goes marching on in the orchards and gardens of the world. Great apples are like great music – they happen rather seldom, but their performance can be ruined by a poor conductor and an under-rehearsed orchestra.

Planting apples and pears

The place for fruit trees is at the bottom of the garden, partly because you will be fetching vegetables every day from the kitchen garden, and your fruit less often, but also because you can see the blossom better from the bedroom windows. Standard apples, pears and plums (if you risk the birds) need to go sixteen feet (5m) apart each way, and ten (3m) from each row end, which allows a maximum of two rows of four in the bottom seventy-four (22m) feet of the average semi-detached house garden. Bush trees are cheaper and on a dwarfing stock such as Malling IX, or M.M. 106 (which not only keeps trees small but gives resistance to woolly aphid), they can go ten feet (3m) apart each way and six (2m) at row ends. This allows three rows of six in seventy-two (21m) feet, if you cut out the central path down the middle of the garden.

If you order your standards early while there is still a choice, ask for 'extra tall', for nothing is worse when you are near six feet (2m) tall, than to have to duck each time you mow under the trees. Choose standards with 6-7 feet (about 2 metres) from the soil mark on the trunk that shows how deep they were planted in the nursery, to the spread of the first branches. Each tree, bush or standard needs a square yard (1m) of bed round it which can be planted with daffodils, but not much else can grow there. Half-standard trees need the same spacing, and are excellent

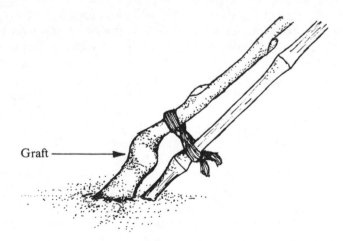

Graft

15 Plant cordons on the slant with key to keep the graft above ground so they cannot 'undwarf' by rooting from above the dwarfing stock.

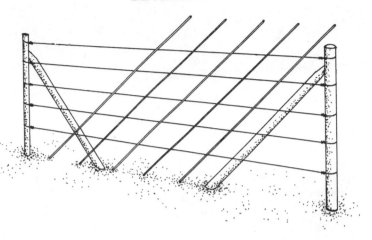

16 Cordons pack the most fruit into least space. They need stout posts
and wires with 7 ft (2.15 m) bamboo canes to train along.

for running chickens under as they keep the crop out of pecking
range.

Dwarf pyramid apples produce the greatest weight of crop off
the smallest space, and as they start as 'maidens' or one-year-old
grafted trees, these are cheaper and do not require the structure
of support posts demanded by cordons – the other system of
packing maximum fruit into minimum space. They are planted
four feet (1m20) apart and nine (3m) between rows, which
should run north and south so the sunlight falls along them. The
space between the trees is left bare, a six-foot (2m) strip is
grassed down and mown between rows, and the apples grow as
a kind of fruiting hedge about seven feet (2m) high. They are
grown on dwarfing stocks and summer pruned as described for
July.

Dig the holes well in advance, two feet (60cm) square and
eighteen inches (45cm) deep, fork up the bottom and drive
home the stakes before planting as recommended earlier. Bush
trees need short, stout stakes to come up as far as the fork of the
branches, and dwarf pyramids need one that reaches about four
feet (1m20) above ground level. Remove the subsoil from the
bottom of the planting hole and replace with better soil, even if
you have to buy turf, because nothing repays a good start more
than apples and pears.

These trees are not in such need of lime as stone fruit, but

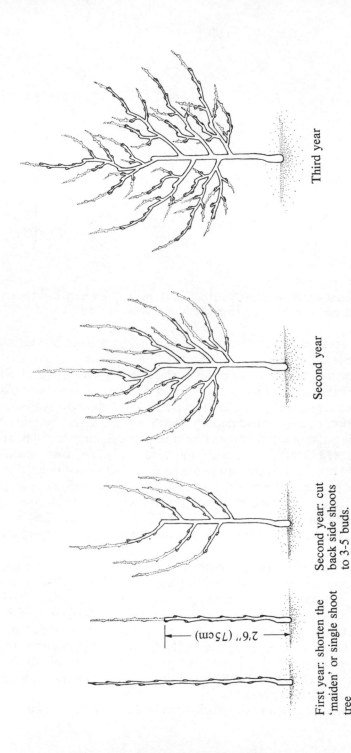

First year: shorten the 'maiden' or single shoot tree

2'6" (75cm)

Second year: cut back side shoots to 3-5 buds.

Second year

Third year

17 Dwarf pyramid pear/apple pruning

they do need magnesium so, instead of chicken grit, spread 2 lb (1 kg) of dolomite in each hole, with bonemeal and hoof and horn. On sandy soils add 2 lb (1 kg) a hole of rock potash, for trees stay a long time in one place and appreciate a slowly released hoard of lasting minerals.

Standard and bush trees can be bought ready pruned, and if you ask when ordering in August or September, the nursery will have time to make a note to have this done. If not, cut back the smooth-barked wood that grew the previous summer by a third, finishing on a bud that points outwards, and shorten half the lesser branches or laterals to 2-3 inches (5-8cm). Dwarf pyramids should be pruned as in the diagram. Make sure when shortening the leaders in winter that the central main leader is well above the others.

It takes two people to plant a tree, one to hold it and fit the roots spread on the bottom of the hole round the stake, and the other to fill back the soil carefully, working it among the roots and waiting to tread it until there is enough soil over the roots for your shoes not to damage the bark. Cut off the ends of any broken roots cleanly and be sure that the bulge which shows where the tree was grafted is well above ground level. It can root direct into the soil and 'undwarf' itself.

A choice of apples

Apples are the nicest source of easily storable Vitamin C that can be grown in every garden, and offer all the minerals that are found in cider vinegar, which itself is a 'locker-up' of this important vitamin. They vary in how much they hold, as well as in taste, storing qualities, blossoming period and many other qualities. Table 16 is based on *Nutritional Values in Crops and Plants* by Professor Werner Schuphan (Faber and Faber, 1965).

Northern Spy is sometimes imported from the USA and is a bargain in bought Vitamin C, compared with Rome Beauty which is frequently in the shops. Golden Delicious is only 2.5 mg behind our Cox, but the difference in taste is as that between Coca Cola and good wine. It also needs a warmer climate than ours for full production, so even those who like it cannot grow it well themselves. The highest Vitamin C cooker is Golden Noble, but when cooked, an apple's Vitamin C content is halved, so it comes down to a level between Cox and Lane's Prince Albert, but this is still far ahead of Bramley's Seedling,

Table 16: Average Vitamin C content in apples

(E = Eater; C = Cooker)	Vitamin C Mg per 100g
Ribston Pippin (E)	30.60
Sturmer Pippin (E)	29.00
Golden Noble (C)	25.10
Orleans Reinette (E)	22.40
King of the Pippins (E)	18.10
Reinette du Canada (C or E)	17.20
Northern Spy (E)	16.70
Adams' Pearmain (E)	16.30
Bramley Seedling (C or E)	16.00
White Transparent (C or E)	15.30
Beauty of Bath (E)	14.00
Peasgood's Nonsuch (C or E)	13.20
Blenheim Orange (C or E)	13.20
Lane's Prince Albert (C)	12.70
Cox's Orange Pippin (E)	10.50
Gascoyne's Scarlet (C or E)	8.90
Worcester Pearmain (E)	8.20
Golden Delicious (E)	8.20
Bismark (C)	7.90
Court Pendu Plat (E)	7.50
Allington Pippin (E)	7.30
James Grieve (E)	6.80
Edward VII (C)	6.30
Laxton's Superb (E)	5.10
Early Victoria (C)	4.80
Rome Beauty (E)	3.80

which comes down to just below Golden Delicious.

If you have room for only one apple, choose Allington Pippin *(Oct.-Dec.)*, which is one of the few self-fertile varieties, a good cooker as well as an acid and aromatic eater with a taste of Cox (one of its parents), and with a place above the bottom of the Vitamin C league table. It is hardy, vigorous and a heavy cropper, with the added advantage that it will pollinate Cox well, for it blossoms at the same time, and if you decide you have room for another, you can have a Cox to go with it. Its eating season begins rather earlier, as shown by the months after its name and because it is a vigorous tree it should be grafted on M.M. 106. If there is room at the bottom of your garden to plant it fifteen feet (5 m) from the end fence, have a standard rather than a dwarf pyramid, on Malling II.

Those who live in the far north, with a short growing season and late frosts, should choose Crawley Beauty *(Dec.-Feb.)* which also fruits alone, and is a fine frothy cooker, but will ripen to golden-yellow sweetness. It is the latest apple to blossom and thrives on cold clays. With room for two, plant also Court Pendu Plat *(Dec.-May)* which produces small, yellow-fleshed fruit in quantity on a modestly growing tree, usually handicapped for lack of a pollen partner with the same late, frost-defeating blossom. It is an excellent apple for tough conditions, with about the same Vitamin C as Allington.

For less extreme conditions, north of a line from Birmingham to the Wash, where Cox fails to thrive, choose Laxton's Royalty *(Nov.-Mar.)* which is a cross between Cox and Court Pendu Plat, with the late blossoming of the second parent and almost the flavour of the first. With it plant Winston *(Jan.-Mar.)*, a good flavour eater, a strong grower and resistant to scab, as well as a late-blossoming frost dodger. With room for a third, make this Gascoyne's Scarlet *(Sept.-Jan.)*, a vigorous tree, with soft, red-tinted flesh, and a good eater with a flavour, next to Cox on Vitamin C. It is perhaps the best apple for a chalky soil, where Winston is also excellent. The two make an ideal couple for chalky gardens where they should ideally be grafted on Malling II, because Malling IX does not give them sufficient root-hold against winds that blow over big beaches. To make a fourth, add King of the Pippins *(Oct.-Dec.)*, with a slightly bitter-sweet taste, a heavy crop, scab resistance and excellent Vitamin C, and a good companion for Laxton's Royalty. Apple planting is not like collecting stamps – choose any two out of a group and add 25 per cent of any other as commercial growers do if you have the room.

The high Vitamin C group all flower rather earlier than Cox or James Grieve, our two most popular apples. They are apples for the south and this is why they are not in every garden. The highest of all is Ribston Pippin *(Nov.-Jan.)* with a superb flavour, crisp, juicy and aromatic, but reputed to do best with *two* pollinators. Plant it with Adams' (not Worcester) Pearmain *(Dec.-Mar.)* with a 'Coxy' flavour and more Vitamin C, and Egremont Russet *(Oct.-Dec.)*, which has a good flavour, upright habit, and the russet-brown skin of this type of apple.

For an early eater in place of any other group, choose Merton Charm *(Sept.-Oct.)*, which is better flavoured than James Grieve and keeps better, but is new and scarce. Use the Henry Doubleday Research Association Fruit Finder Service for this or anything uncommon and not to be found in garden centres.

Sturmer Pippin is only 1.60 mg behind the winner and blossoms just right to pollinate Cox. It is a good cropper, a nice eater and a compact grower, which should be left to ripen on the tree as long as possible. Cox's Orange Pippin *(Dec.-May)* is the finest-flavoured apple of all, but needs a well-drained soil (not a cold, wet clay) and a watch kept to see it does not run out of magnesium – the key sign is whether the leaves drop early but stay on at the tips of the young shoots. Spray with Epsom salts as suggested earlier or use dolomite at planting time or as a surface dressing. Rock potash is also appreciated, but chemical nitrogen leads to scab and canker.

As a pollinator for Cox, or for Sturmer Pippin (if you decide to be original and *not* plant Cox), James Grieve *(Sept.-Oct.)* is an early eater, but not a good keeper. Another with a flavour similar to Cox but much more resistant to cold is Kidd's Orange Red *(Nov.-Feb.)* which resists scab and mildew.

Among the leaders on Vitamin C is Orleans Reinette *(Dec.-Feb.)*, a famous apple for flavour, good in the north and partly self-fertile, but it crops better with another late-blossoming kind. It is liable to scab and canker, but is mainly unpopular because its blossom period does not fit Cox. Plant it with Golden Noble, which will ripen for eating although on the sharp side, or Duke of Devonshire *(Jan.-Mar.)*, which is firm, yellow and sweet, a good compact grower for small gardens and highly scab resisting.

A choice of pears

Pears are delicious, but need to be eaten when they are still juicy and mellow, before they go 'sleepy' or overripe. We are spoiled by being able to buy pears from cool storage almost all the year round, and have lost the art of judging the colour shade and softness that meant each variety was exactly right to eat with silver fruit knives. They are lower in Vitamin C than apples, ranging from 4-7 mg like plums, and they blossom earlier, so are more likely to catch frosts. As far as we know, no one has ever been allergic to pears so those concerned with allergy should plant pear trees.

We are rapidly becoming a one-pear country, for the excellent in horticulture is always the enemy of choice, and Conference, the long, tapered pear that everyone knows, has got everything for the amateur gardener, and nearly everything for the commercial grower. It is self-fertile, a strong grower, a heavy cropper, sweet and juicy and is at its best in October and November.

The only other pear we have that is holding its own is Doyenné du Comice *(Nov.)*, with a better flavour but susceptible to scab. It needs a pollinator and since Laxton's Superb got firelight and had to be destroyed to prevent this bacterial disease which came from America, killing all the pears in Britain, the best is Buerre Hardy *(Oct.)*. This is a vigorous, heavy cropper with a fine flavour, and autumn leaves that are a splendid red.

Dr Jules Guyot *(Sept.)* is also self-fertile with a better flavour than Conference and as heavy a cropper, but resisting scab. Another self-fertile pear is Margaret Marillat *(Sept.)*, also a heavy cropper, rather like Conference in appearance but not such a good flavour, though sweet and juicy.

Choose your apples and pears with care, for you are buying thirty to fifty years of fruit and blossom; the price you pay for your trees will be doubled, if you accept a substitute from the nursery's stock which catches the frost in your garden and you then have to buy another. Unlike potatoes, which you can try new each year till you find the one that suits your taste and conditions, fruit trees are like good marriages – they can, with careful cultivation, grow in splendour of blossom, richness and delight in your garden, as long as you both shall live.

Appendix

The Henry Doubleday Research Association

The Henry Doubleday Research Association began in 1955 out of a book, a bear and a ton of lucerne seed. The book was my *Russian Comfrey* (now long out of print), which began modern comfrey growing in all countries, and the HDRA grew out of the fan mail it drew from farmers and gardeners all round the world.

In 1954 I sent the first modern comfrey from Mrs Greer's field to Canada, and Mr A. H. A. Lasker, the Canadian seedsman who bought it, sent me a ton of lucerne seed as a gift for my part in the epic struggle that got it across.

The lucerne was a variety barred to Britain by dollar shortage and about the most awkward possible present for a struggling gardening writer, for it hit Regulation 365, which then controlled food parcels and laid down that gifts must weigh no more than 22 lb (10 kg) and be 'for personal use only'. Such use would have required 50 acres (20 hectares) on which to sow the seed, and stock to eat it; but the £275 that a famous farm seedsman was willing to pay for it would be enough to start a research station.

Two MPs fought hard to get it through. There was a letter in the *New Statesman*, and an article in *Time and Tide* – but all in vain. Canada's gift lay at the London docks awaiting a British 'Boston Tea Party' – until a second generous gift arrived at the Regulation 365 barrier.

While the battle of the seed was raging, an American wild-animal dealer gave a nice, tame, black bear to an old friend in

London, whose wife objected to its 'personal use' as a pet. Two hundredweight (100kg) of bear, breaking the weight restriction, sitting up to beg dockers' sandwiches and posing with Teddy-bear appeal for Fleet Street photographers, ' soon crashed through the red-tape barrier. So it ambled to the children's corner of a zoo, closely pursued through the dock gates by a ton of lucerne seed.

With the money from selling the seed, I leased the Trial Ground at £10 a year when it was only ¾ of an acre (0.3 hectares), paid for the fencing, the labour cost of planting the comfrey presented by the Comfrey Growers of Britain, and the publication of *Comfrey Report No. 1* (also now out of print). From that small beginning we have grown, until in 1958 we became a Registered Charity of the type that gives away knowledge rather than money.

We would now be homeless had we not in 1961 appealed to our members (then only 470) and raised £1,500 towards the £2,500 needed to buy the freehold at building-land price. Then a member of our committee, the late Dr Sidney Osborn of Ipswich, lent us £1,000, interest-free, to acquire the land for ever, with a long triangle reaching down towards a bird sanctuary and giving us just two acres (0.8 hectares). To our great regret, Dr Osborn died that winter, before we had begun paying back his loan, and left us the balance in his will. So, in part, our Trial Ground is a memorial to the doctor who bought the infant HDRA into the world, and to the generosity of our members in many countries.

I christened the Association after Henry Doubleday (1813-1902) who was a Quaker, like his forbears who sailed with William Penn to Pennsylvania. One of his descendants founded Doubleday's, the American publisher, and his cousin Henry Doubleday of Epping made the first collection of butterflies for the British Museum. Henry Doubleday of Coggeshall introduced the hybrid he called 'Russian comfrey' from Russia in the 1870s, in the hope that its protein (called 'mucilaginous matter' in some of the early analyses) would replace the erratic supplies of gum arabic that were endangering his contract with the firm of De la Rue to supply gum for the later penny-black stamps and some of the early colonial issues.

Unfortunately, gummy proteins do not stick stamps; Henry lost his contract, and his small gum factory failed. He appears to have introduced an F_1 hybrid of comfrey which produced up to 100 tonnes an acre in Britain, and to have spent the last thirty years of his life experimenting with it. It was his dream that the crop would not only feed horses, cattle, sheep, pigs and poultry, but also solve the problem of world hunger, when that vision came not from biologist Paul Ehrlich but from the Irish Potato Famine of the 1840s. After his death, his relations cleared up after 'poor Uncle Henry', the dedicated elderly bachelor, and burned the records of his work. As I was determined that my work on comfrey, which began in 1948, should not be tidied away and lost, I founded the Association and named it in his honour.

The work of the Association soon grew far beyond the agricultural, horticultural, medicinal and nutritional uses of comfrey, and it has gone on growing until today it is the largest body in what is loosely called 'The Organic Movement' in Britain, and the third largest in the world. Its official objects are:

1 The improvement and encouragement of agriculture and horticulture generally.

2 Research into, and the study of, improved methods of organic farming and gardening.

3 Research into the utilization of Russian comfrey in connection with the foregoing objects.

4 The encouragement of research and experiment in agriculture and horticulture by, and the dissemination of knowledge of the results of such research and experiment among, farmers, gardeners and schools.

5. The advancement of knowledge of, and the fostering of public interest in, the benefits to be derived from the utilization of Russian Comfrey and other plants useful in organic husbandry.

It is a Research Association because a proportion of its members carry out experiments in their own gardens, as a hobby. These experiments are designed to find cheap, simple and effective answers to the problems of gardening using the fewest chemicals. Because this kind of research rarely has any prospect of finding anything to patent or sell, and is rarely carried out even by universities, it is still possible for amateurs to step over the frontiers of science beside their garden paths.

The design of the experiments is carried out at the Trial Ground, and though many start from 'old wives' tales', still more often begin with a search through scientific papers by the HDRA staff, to find a possible way round an awkward pest problem.

Today, when as much as 80 per cent of a gardening work can be adapted from other books or, in the organic field, copied from those written for other countries with different pests, diseases, crops and climates, there is an ever-increasing demand for knowledge based on practical experience and sound research. In 1982, two hundred and sixty of our six thousand five hundred members took part in this type of experiment, which can become an absorbing interest for any keen gardener. But experimenters form only a small percentage of an association which anyone can join, for a subscription in 1983 of £8 a year or, for pensioners, £4 (though inflation and, especially, increases in postage rates, raise this slowly as time passes), and members range from complete beginners with their first garden to Ph.Ds in the varied subjects covered by our work. Most members, however, join in order to receive the Association's quarterly newsletter, and to benefit from its gardening advisory service, as well as to support what has been described as 'the growing point of the organic movement'.

The Trial Ground at Bocking, with four Open Days in July and August, has now become almost an organic mini-Wisley. Its resources include a library, available for research and study, which is mainly used at present by the four students a year who are the small number the Association has the space to train, trial plots that test out the many new systems of organic gardening, and experiments in the field of fertility, on which much of this book has been based.

The Association has a number of local groups spread over the British Isles, three in Australia, one in New Zealand and one in India, which has just founded the first organic Farming Institute in a tropical country. A recent development is a vigorous campaign to preserve the vanishing vegetable varieties, which are just as important a part of our genetic heritage as our equally endangered wild life. 'Vegetable Sanctuaries', in which they can be preserved as though they were birds or wild flowers, are being started in Britain and overseas, where the need is more urgent because so many more species are in peril.

The scope of the HDRA has extended beyond gardening

compost heaps and companion plants to population, pollution, diet and nutrition, because the concern of its members is for the Organic Movement as a whole. We grow, we change, we learn, we correct our mistakes and above all we think ahead, drawing the line between 'organic' and 'inorganic' – between all that which we can enjoy out of the income of the good earth, and that which will harm those who will still need to use and love our land when we are gone.

If you are interested in learning more about the Association, or have difficulty in obtaining any of the fruit varieties, seeds, organic fertilizer, biological pest or disease controls or any other product mentioned in this book, please write to this address, enclosing a stamped, addressed envelope.

The Henry Doubleday Research Association,
Convent Lane,
Bocking,
Braintree, Essex CM7 6RW

Index